The Who Was?

HISTORY OF THE WORLD

DELUXE EDITION

The Who Was?

HISTORY OF THE WORLD

DELUXE EDITION

by Paula K. Manzanero

illustrations by Robert Squier, Nancy Harrison, and others

Penguin Workshop

To my favorite history buff:
Marie K. in PA,
my mom—PKM

For Stanley and Stanley—one a witness of the past,
the other a witness to the future—RS

PENGUIN WORKSHOP
An Imprint of Penguin Random House LLC, New York

Copyright © 2019 by Penguin Random House LLC. All rights reserved.
Previously published in 2019 by Penguin Workshop.
This deluxe edition published in 2021 by Penguin Workshop,
an imprint of Penguin Random House LLC, New York.
PENGUIN and PENGUIN WORKSHOP are trademarks
of Penguin Books Ltd. WHO HQ & Design is a registered trademark of
Penguin Random House LLC. Manufactured in China.

Visit us online at www.penguinrandomhouse.com.

Library of Congress Control Number: 2019947149

ISBN 9780593224342   10 9 8 7 6 5 4 3 2 1

ello, history buffs and Who Was? fans! Did you know that planet Earth is around 4.6 billion years old? Humans had already developed tools, fire, and the art of cave painting loooong before King Tut was born. The first farmers were growing crops, keeping animals, and establishing villages and towns. *The Who Was? History of the World* is a journey along the timeline of history, noting when 150 of the subjects in our series first arrived (Happy Birthday to all!) and what was happening in the world at that moment in time. Follow along to learn who was doing what when, from the days of ancient Egypt, all the way up to the present.

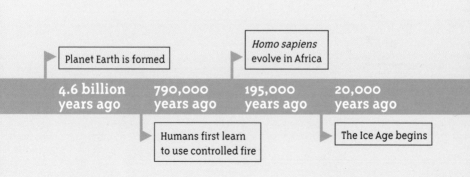

Planet Earth is formed		*Homo sapiens* evolve in Africa	
4.6 billion years ago	**790,000 years ago**	**195,000 years ago**	**20,000 years ago**
	Humans first learn to use controlled fire		The Ice Age begins

ncient Egypt was a mighty civilization that lasted for three thousand years, from around 3100 BCE* until 30 BCE. In the Valley of the Kings, along the Nile River, the Egyptians built massive pyramids and temples to honor their pharaohs, queens, and royal families.

* This stands for "Before the Common Era." See page 7 for details.

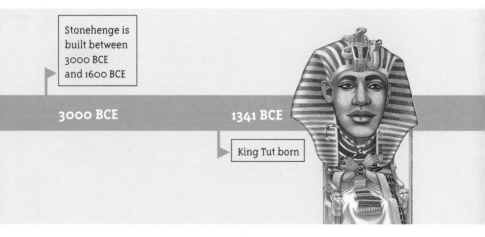

Stonehenge is built between 3000 BCE and 1600 BCE

3000 BCE

1341 BCE

King Tut born

The Olmecs are the first city-based civilization in Central America

1200 BCE   **776 BCE**

Ancient Greeks hold their first games at Olympia

It only took Alexander the Great, one of the greatest military leaders in history, a little over ten years to conquer existing empires and establish his own huge kingdom. It covered most of the then-known world, from India to Egypt.

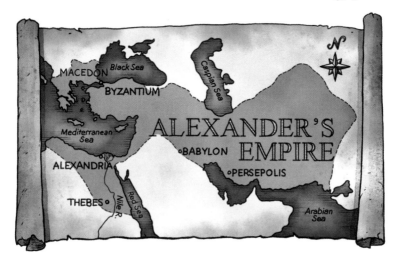

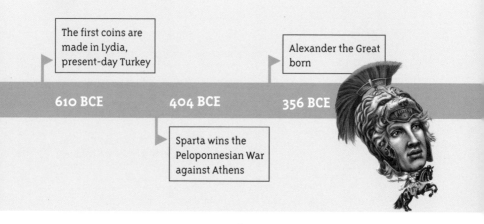

The first coins are made in Lydia, present-day Turkey

Alexander the Great born

610 BCE   **404 BCE**   **356 BCE**

Sparta wins the Peloponnesian War against Athens

Alexander, who was born in Pella, Macedon (present-day Greece), carried the Greek language and culture with him. And he loved to name cities after himself! Here are just a few of the many "Alexander" cities and their present-day locations. There are over seventy in total!

- Alexandria (Egypt)
- Alexandria Ariana (Afghanistan)
- Alexandria Carmania (Iran)
- Alexandria Eschate (Tajikistan)
- Alexandria Orietai (Pakistan)
- Alexandria on the Caucasus (Afghanistan)
- Alexandria on the Indus (Pakistan)

The Great Wall of China is begun, when Emperor Qin Shi Huang connects earlier fortifications to protect his new dynasty

350 BCE   **C. 221 BCE**

Nazca culture of Peru begins

When Julius Caesar said, "I came, I saw, I conquered," he wasn't kidding. By the time Jesus was born, Caesar had been dead for over forty years. But during Jesus's lifetime, the Romans controlled a huge empire thanks to Caesar's expansion plan. The Roman Empire included land all around the Mediterranean Sea, from Spain, France, and parts of North Africa to Turkey and Syria.

Over two thousand years ago, Jesus was born in a stable in Bethlehem, in what is now Palestine. His followers called him "Christ," which means "savior." Centuries later, Christian monks—

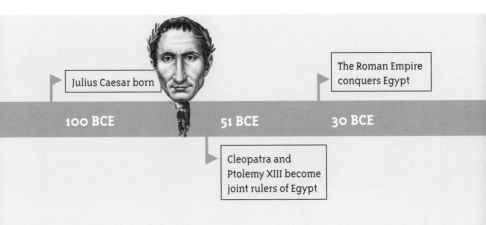

Julius Caesar born

The Roman Empire conquers Egypt

100 BCE   51 BCE   30 BCE

Cleopatra and Ptolemy XIII become joint rulers of Egypt

Christ's followers—developed a calendar that called anything that happened before Jesus's birth "BC," meaning *before Christ.* And they counted those years backward from year one.

Because they wrote their accounts in Latin, the monks abbreviated *anno Domini*—in the year of the Lord—as "AD." So anything that happened *after* the birth of Jesus (that would be anything after year one) was noted as "AD."

But today, we also use the terms "BCE" meaning "before the Common Era" and "CE" for the "Common Era." It can be confusing! But the dividing line is still year one.

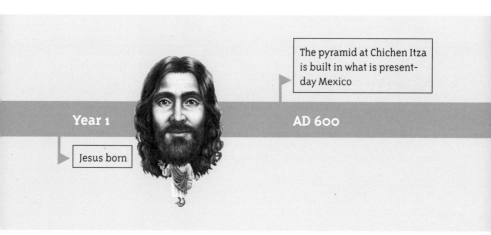

The pyramid at Chichen Itza is built in what is present-day Mexico

Year 1

AD 600

Jesus born

7

By the time Leif Erikson arrived in the Americas at Newfoundland, Canada, around 1001, the classic era of the Maya civilization—far to the south—was already over. Deep in the jungles

of Central America, the Maya had already developed a complete system of writing, a sophisticated calendar, and a mastery of math and astronomy.

The Maya glyph—or symbol—for zero was a shell.

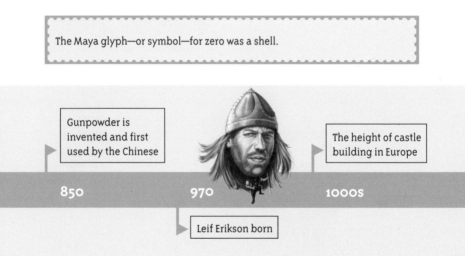

Gunpowder is invented and first used by the Chinese

The height of castle building in Europe

850

970

1000S

Leif Erikson born

In 1215, the noble barons of England forced King John to sign the Magna Carta (that's Latin for "Great Charter"). They were demanding a contract that guaranteed justice under the law—an important first step  in protecting against any cruel or unreasonable actions of kings. The establishment of the rule of law was the basis for all future democracies.

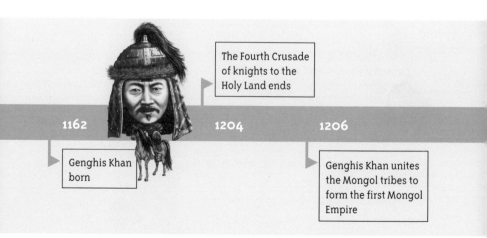

The Fourth Crusade of knights to the Holy Land ends

1162

1204

1206

Genghis Khan born

Genghis Khan unites the Mongol tribes to form the first Mongol Empire

The Silk Road

The Silk Road spanned over four thousand miles from the Mediterranean Sea in the west to China in the east. From 200 BCE to 1400 CE, it was the most important trade route in the world. All sorts of products traveled in both directions. Food, wine, salt, and glassware were sent east. And silk, paper, and gunpowder were carried west.

Marco Polo, an Italian who wrote about his journeys on the Silk Road in 1298, was its most famous traveler. While young Marco was coming

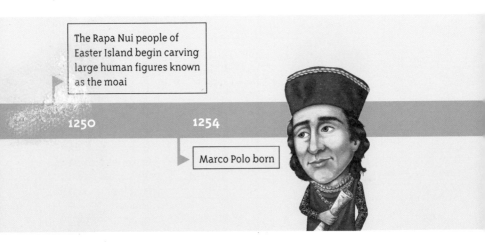

The Rapa Nui people of Easter Island begin carving large human figures known as the moai

1250   1254

Marco Polo born

and going, the Mongolian Empire, founded by Genghis Khan, had already reached the height of its power and influence in 1279.

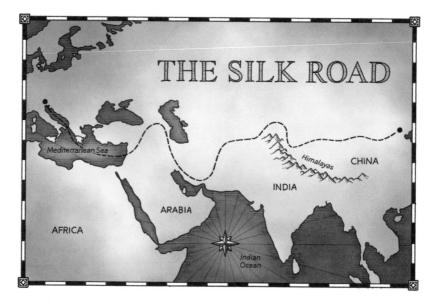

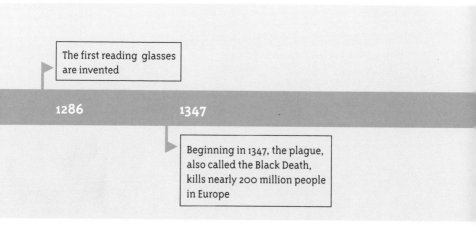

The first reading glasses are invented

1286   **1347**

Beginning in 1347, the plague, also called the Black Death, kills nearly 200 million people in Europe

The Hundred Years' War

The Hundred Years' War was a series of conflicts between France and England that lasted from the 1330s to the 1450s. It wasn't fought steadily for one hundred years, but still: That was a long time to be at war. After many battles and raids, Joan of Arc led French troops to an important victory at Orleans in 1429.

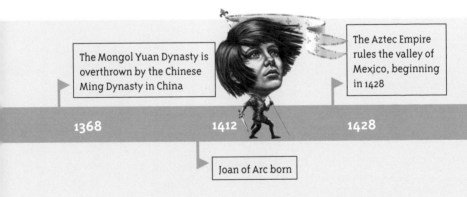

The Mongol Yuan Dynasty is overthrown by the Chinese Ming Dynasty in China

The Aztec Empire rules the valley of Mexico, beginning in 1428

1368

1412

1428

Joan of Arc born

The English Longbow

Invented around 1200, the English longbow was a great help to the English in their battles against the French. It was longer and much more powerful than ordinary bows of the time.

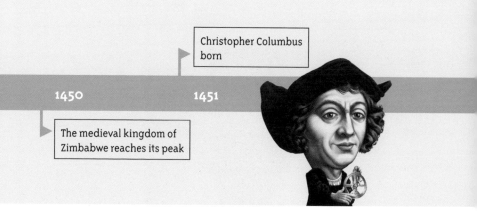

Christopher Columbus born

1450   1451

The medieval kingdom of Zimbabwe reaches its peak

The Renaissance (1300–1650)

The ancient Greek statue known as the Venus de Milo

The Renaissance began in Italy in the 1300s and spread throughout Europe. It signaled a new appreciation for the classic ideas of ancient Greece and Rome. Artists like Leonardo da Vinci still painted religious subjects, which was expected at the time. But they also wanted to show the beauty of nature and the human body as

Leonardo da Vinci born

1452

well, just as the ancient cultures had.

William Shakespeare, born in 1564, was one of the first playwrights to show the human side of his characters—to show people as they truly are, bringing the core ideas of the Renaissance to the theater. He wrote plays about sometimes flawed people and their everyday lives. Shakespeare saw the beauty in human nature, even with all its imperfections. ·

"The human foot is a masterpiece of engineering and a work of art."
—Leonardo da Vinci

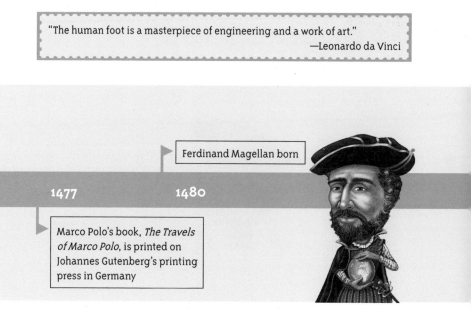

Ferdinand Magellan born

1477   1480

Marco Polo's book, *The Travels of Marco Polo*, is printed on Johannes Gutenberg's printing press in Germany

The Age of Exploration

The Age of Exploration was at its peak from the late 1400s until around 1597. Europeans set out to find new trade routes. They developed the skills and equipment to sail long distances and, in the process, arrived in new worlds. The Portuguese, under the leadership of Prince Henry the Navigator, played a large role in mapping and colonizing during the Age of Exploration.

Henry VIII born

1491

Famous Portuguese Navigators

enry the Navigator (1394–1460) founded a scientific school of navigation.

Vasco da Gama (1469–1524) was the first to sail around the southern tip of Africa.

Henry the Navigator

Ferdinand Magellan's expedition was the first to sail all the way around the world, heading west to reach the East.

Leonardo da Vinci completes his painting *Mona Lisa*

1492

1506

The Inca Empire in South America has a population close to 15 million

Christopher Columbus reaches the New World, the Americas

The Conquest of the Aztec Empire by the Spanish, Led by Hernán Cortés

The conquistadors were men who sailed from Spain to the New World in the years following the voyages of Columbus. They were seeking fame, but mostly fortune.

Spanish conquistador Hernán Cortés sailed to Central America in 1519. He brought more than five hundred men and eleven ships. After landing on the east coast of Mexico and founding the city

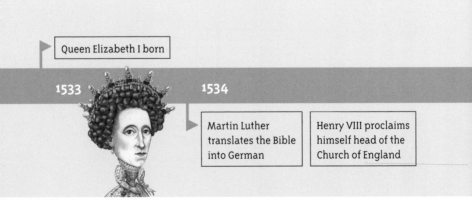

Queen Elizabeth I born

1533

1534

Martin Luther translates the Bible into German

Henry VIII proclaims himself head of the Church of England

of Veracruz, he marched toward the Aztec capital of Tenochtitlán, gathering native people for his army along the way. By the time the capital city fell to the Spaniards in 1521, the Aztec king Montezuma II had already lost the support of his people—and the conquest of the Americas was underway.

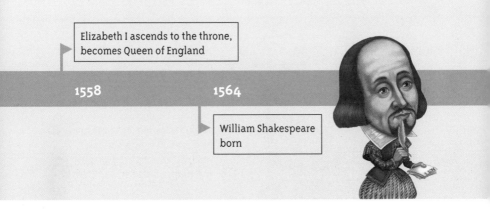

Elizabeth I ascends to the throne, becomes Queen of England

1558

1564

William Shakespeare born

New World Colonies (1624)

As more Europeans traveled westward, their presence in North, Central, and South America grew. The Spanish, English, Dutch, Portuguese, and French took over lands from the Native Americans and established colonies—areas occupied by their own people but under control of their European homelands.

What we think of as colonial America was made up of the thirteen British colonies that were founded between 1607 and 1733 along the northeast coast of what is now the United States.

Galileo born

1564

1632

Galileo is sentenced to life in prison for heresy (having opinions that went against the teachings of the Catholic Church)

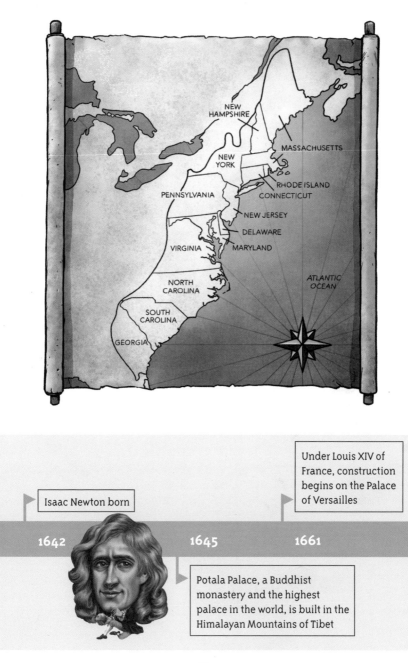

Isaac Newton born

Under Louis XIV of France, construction begins on the Palace of Versailles

1642

1645

1661

Potala Palace, a Buddhist monastery and the highest palace in the world, is built in the Himalayan Mountains of Tibet

Pirates of the Spanish Main

From Florida to Central America and the Caribbean, and down to the northern coast of South America, Spain established colonies in the New World. The Spanish looted tons of gold from their territories—which were known as the Spanish Main—and loaded it onto ships headed east, back to the king and queen of Spain.

These treasure-laden ships were tempting prizes for pirates like Blackbeard, Mary Read, and Henry Morgan. Spanish galleons were often

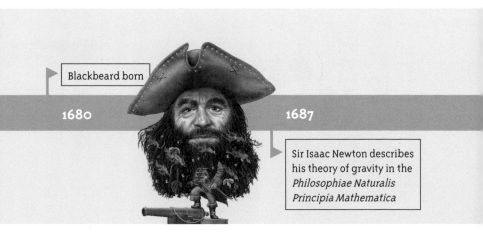

Blackbeard born

1680

1687

Sir Isaac Newton describes his theory of gravity in the *Philosophiae Naturalis Principia Mathematica*

raided in the Caribbean Sea before they could reach the open water of the Atlantic Ocean. The town of Port Royal, Jamaica, and the island of Tortuga were well-known pirate safe havens.

Henry Morgan's ship *Satisfaction*

Ushering in the Age of Reason (1685–1815)

The Enlightenment was a philosophy—a certain way of thinking—that dominated the 1700s. People began to challenge long-held beliefs. And rather than just accepting things as they were, they worked to prove or disprove ideas through scientific experiments and methods. They also began to value the idea of questioning what had always simply been accepted as truth.

As scientific and political debates became more common, so did the idea of rebellion and

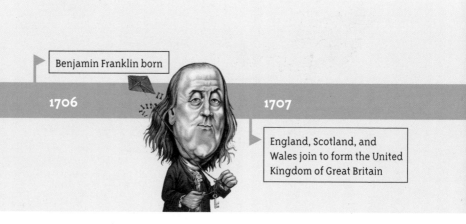

Benjamin Franklin born

1706

1707

England, Scotland, and Wales join to form the United Kingdom of Great Britain

revolution. Everything became open to criticism, including outdated scientific theories, political systems, and the rule of kings.

Translation: Trust No One (Don't take anyone's word for it.)

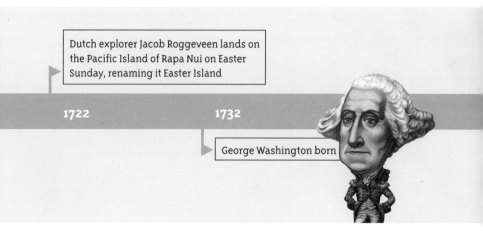

Dutch explorer Jacob Roggeveen lands on the Pacific Island of Rapa Nui on Easter Sunday, renaming it Easter Island

1722   1732

George Washington born

The Triangle of the Slave Trade

The Atlantic slave trade, which lasted from the 1500s through the 1800s, captured twelve million Africans by force to work as slaves in the Americas. Ships leaving the west coast of Africa packed with those who had been captured traveled across the Atlantic Ocean to South, Central, and North America and the Caribbean, where the enslaved Africans labored on cotton and sugar plantations as well as in gold and silver mines. These products, along with tobacco, rum,

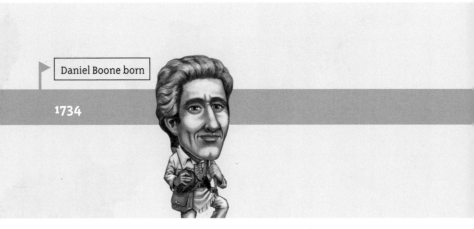

Daniel Boone born

1734

molasses, and other exports, were sent back to countries in Europe. Once emptied of their goods, the French, British, Dutch, Portuguese, and Spanish ships would head to slave ports in Africa, to be refilled with human cargo, thus completing the "triangle of trade."

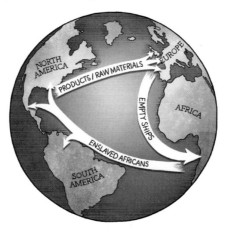

Maria Theresa is crowned Queen of Hungary

1735

1741

Paul Revere born

Girl Power!

In 1740, Maria Theresa became empress of the Habsburg Empire in Europe. She was the only woman to ever rule the empire. Some other (male) European rulers didn't accept her as the true ruler. And France and Prussia united to invade her homeland of Austria. Maria Theresa's fifteenth child, Marie Antoinette, eventually became the last queen of France.

Thomas Jefferson born

1743

Catherine the Great was the empress of Russia from 1762 to 1796. She was Russia's longest-ruling female leader—and she wasn't even Russian! Catherine had been born in Prussia (now Poland) as "Sophia." But she was

beloved by the Russian people, who thought she was just "great."

Catherine the Great established the Smolny Institute in St. Petersburg in 1764. It was the first school in Russia for girls.

Princeton University is founded in New Jersey

1744

1746

Abigail Adams born

Something Electric in the Air . . .

In May 1752, Benjamin Franklin tested the lightning rod. One month later, on June 10, he and his son William demonstrated electricity with a house key and a kite in a thunderstorm.

Betsy Ross born

Benjamin Franklin invents the lightning rod

The Liberty Bell arrives in Philadelphia, Pennsylvania, from its foundry in London, England

1752

Although the kite was not struck by lightni... Franklin's hand caused an electrical spark when he moved it near the key, proving that the nature of lightning is indeed electrical.

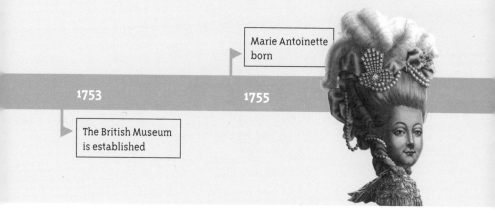

Marie Antoinette born

1753

1755

The British Museum is established

Seven Years' War

The Seven Years' War was a global conflict that drew in every great European power of the time. It was fought in Europe, the Americas, Africa, and Asia! A tangle of alliances and coalitions formed around Great Britain on one side and France on the other. The war changed the political order of Europe and influenced many later events around the globe. Many colonial territories changed hands. Fought from 1756 to 1763, the Seven Years' War is considered to be the first true world war.

Alexander Hamilton born

1755

THE SEVEN YEARS' WAR

BRITISH TERRITORIES AND ALLIES

FRENCH TERRITORIES AND ALLIES

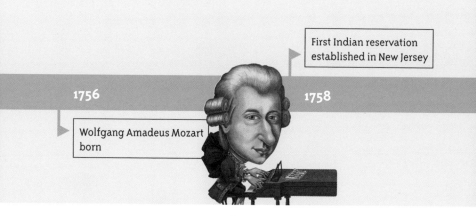

1756

1758

First Indian reservation established in New Jersey

Wolfgang Amadeus Mozart born

The Stamp Act

The British Parliament passed the Stamp Act, the first direct tax asked of people living in the thirteen American colonies, on March 22, 1765. This tax was going to help pay for British military operations in North America.

All official and legal forms were required to carry a stamp proving that the tax had been paid on the printed document. Colonists refused to buy anything that had been imported from Great Britain as a protest. They felt that the Stamp Act violated their political rights. After all, why pay

The Seven Years' War ends

1763

1767

Andrew Jackson born

1769

Napoleon Bonaparte born

taxes to a government (King George III and the British Parliament) that they had no voice in?

Colonial patriots, including Samuel Adams and Patrick Henry, used the rallying cry

King George III
(1738–1820)

"No taxation without representation!" They wanted to keep American colonists focused on their rights and liberties. Although the Stamp Act was repealed in 1766, the repeal was too little, too late. The idea of breaking free of the king's rule had already taken hold.

British colonists in Massachusetts protest taxes by throwing tea into Boston Harbor in what would come to be known as the Boston Tea Party

1770   1773

Captain James Cook claims Australia for England

The Continental Congress

The very first Continental Congress was held in 1774 to figure out the best way to respond to and negotiate with the British Parliament. The Second Continental Congress, held eight months later, on May 10, 1775, formed the Continental Army and named George Washington its commander. A resolution in the second congress called the colonies free and independent states. It also created a committee to write a Declaration of Independence.

Johnny Appleseed born

1774

1775

Battles in Lexington and Concord, Massachusetts, begin the American Revolutionary War

On July 4, 1776, all the delegates, including the document's author, Thomas Jefferson, adopted and signed the Declaration of Independence in Philadelphia, Pennsylvania.

Thomas Paine urges independence from Great Britain for the Thirteen American Colonies in his pamphlet *Common Sense*

1776

Jane Austen born

The American Revolution (1776–1781)

The Continental Army volunteers were facing the well-trained British army—one of the very best in the world. But they knew their own territory well, they had support from many of the colonial civilians, and they were passionate about their cause!

France recognizes the United States of America as an independent nation

1777

1783

The first manned hot-air balloon flight takes place over Paris

It took years of skirmishes, battles, and sieges—
and some help from France and Spain. But on
October 19, 1781, British general Lord George
Cornwallis surrendered to George Washington
in Yorktown, Virginia. Following the surrender,
the British negotiated an end to the American
Revolutionary War.

The Brothers Grimm born

1785, 1786

The French Revolution

The American Revolution ushered in an entire age of revolutions, beginning with the French in 1789. Because the country was nearly bankrupt, King Louis XVI began demanding taxes from even the poorest citizens. The French people saw how extravagantly the king and queen lived. The palace of Versailles alone had 1,400 fountains! Its Hall of Mirrors contained 357 mirrors to reflect the palace gardens!

In July 1789, an angry mob attacked the

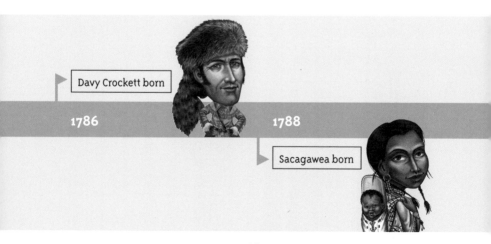

Davy Crockett born

1786

1788

Sacagawea born

Bastille prison in Paris. The people declared a revolution against the king. In 1792, the king lost control of his country and a new government was put in place. It declared France to be a republic. And by the fall of 1793, both Louis XVI and his queen, Marie Antoinette, had been executed by the French people.

Palace of Versailles

The US Congress approves the Bill of Rights—the first ten amendments to the US Constitution

1791

1793

First voluntary immigrants from Britain move to Australia as Free Settlers

The Empire Builder

Two short years after the end of the French Revolution, Napoleon Bonaparte was put in charge of the French army in Italy. And only three years later, he was ruling all of France. In 1804, he was crowned emperor. For the next ten years, he fought battle after battle that left him—and France—controlling much of Europe.

Napoleon was a brilliant strategist who felt that nothing was impossible. And for Napoleon, it seemed to be true. Until his disastrous retreat from Russia in 1812 and his ultimate defeat at

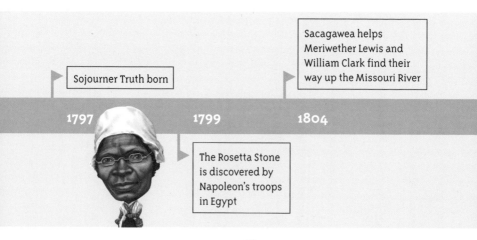

Sojourner Truth born

Sacagawea helps Meriwether Lewis and William Clark find their way up the Missouri River

1797   1799   1804

The Rosetta Stone is discovered by Napoleon's troops in Egypt

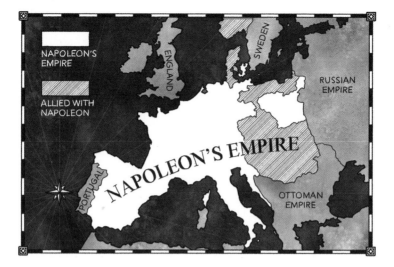

ENGLAND

SWEDEN

RUSSIAN EMPIRE

NAPOLEON'S EMPIRE

PORTUGAL

OTTOMAN EMPIRE

Waterloo in 1815, Napoleon ruled a vast empire and lived up to his many nicknames, including "The Man of Destiny" and the "Colossus of the Nineteenth Century."

1807

Robert E. Lee born

Britain bans the slave trade

Fueling the Future

On February 11, 1808, Jesse Fell of Wilkes-Barre, Pennsylvania, first experimented with burning anthracite coal as fuel. The density and purity of this type of coal made it burn longer and at higher temperatures than other types of coal. This discovery eventually led to the use of coal as the main fuel source of the Industrial Revolution.

Coal could be used to heat huge amounts of water to produce steam. And steam created the power that kept factories and mines running. It

Louis Braille born

1809

also fueled steam-powered locomotive engines (trains) that were essential to the transportation and manufacturing industries.

Edgar Allan Poe born

Territory of Illinois (which also includes present-day Wisconsin and parts of Minnesota and Michigan) is established

The War of 1812

As the new nation of the United States moved to expand its territories beyond the original thirteen colonies, conflicts with Native Americans became more numerous. At this time, the British controlled the Canadian territories. And they were happy to become allies with some native tribes to fight the United States.

Britain waged major attacks on Washington, DC, and Fort McHenry in Baltimore, Maryland. After they lost the Battle of Lake Champlain, near Plattsburgh, New York, the British finally reached

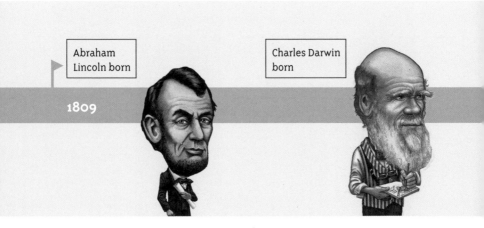

Abraham Lincoln born

Charles Darwin born

1809

an agreement with the Americans.

The War of 1812—which lasted until 1814, or 1815 if you consider that the Battle of New Orleans happened *after* the war officially ended—is also known as "America's Second War for Independence" because it proved that the United States could stand its ground and remain independent from Great Britain.

Grimms' Fairy Tales

Just five days before Christmas in 1812, brothers Jacob and Wilhelm Grimm published eighty-six fairy tales in a brand-new book: *Children's and Household Tales.* Before the Grimms' book, families told folktales around the evening fire, and villagers listened to traveling storytellers. Jacob and Wilhelm wanted to remind people of the hidden treasures—the old stories—of their German culture. They had been collecting the stories for six long years.

The brothers went on to publish a second

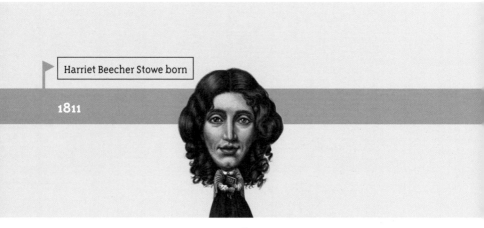

Harriet Beecher Stowe born

1811

volume of *Household Tales* and, eventually, an illustrated English translation. Their stories of Cinderella—whom they called *Ashputtel* in German—Rapunzel, the Frog King, the Golden Goose, and others became world famous. And their success story has provided the world with many happily-ever-afters.

The Grimms were famous for more than just fairy tales. The brothers also published books about medieval studies, mythology, and language. They also started work on a German dictionary. But both died before they reached the letter *G*.

1812

Charles Dickens born

Napoleon's forces invade Russia on June 24 and retreat from Russia on December 14

South American Independence

Napoleon's wars with Portugal and Spain left both countries with a weaker grasp on their colonies in South America. Rebel leader Simón Bolívar—with the help of Haitian leaders—declared Venezuela independent from Spain in 1811 and took over Colombia in 1819. José de San Martín had been fighting for freedom in Argentina and Chile. Bolívar teamed up with him to free Peru and Uruguay. By 1825, Paraguay and Bolivia were also independent. Brazil declared its independence from Portugal in 1822.

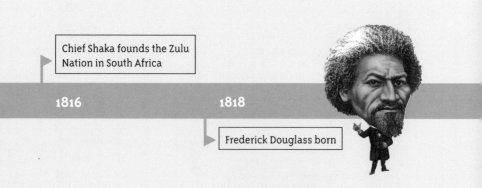

Chief Shaka founds the Zulu Nation in South Africa

1816

1818

Frederick Douglass born

Simón Bolívar (1783–1830)

Simón José Antonio de la Santísima Trinidad de Bolívar y Palacios was known simply as "El Libertador." He was a Venezuelan political and military leader who heroically helped free countries in South America from Spanish rule.

It's Alive!

Mary Shelley (1797–1851)

It was a dark and stormy night when teenage Mary Shelley first thought of the idea for her book *Frankenstein*. The British author was only twenty years old when the book was first published in 1818.

A few years earlier, she had traveled to Germany and stayed near the Frankenstein Castle, an actual German castle overlooking the city of Darmstadt.

Queen Victoria born

1819

And during a competition among friends to see who could write the best horror story, she was inspired to create her early masterpiece about a mad scientist obsessed with creating life.

1820

Susan B. Anthony born

American writer Washington Irving publishes *The Legend of Sleepy Hollow*, America's first ghost story

The Missouri
Compromise of 1820

In 1817, there were twenty-two states in the Union: eleven free states and eleven where slavery was legal. When the Missouri Territory applied for statehood, it asked to be a slaveholding state. The US Senate was afraid that the balance of power in the US government would be tipped toward slavery if the request was granted.

Henry Clay, a representative from Kentucky, had a solution to allow Missouri in as a slave state while establishing Maine as a free state.

Harriet Tubman born

c. 1820

Slavery would then become illegal anywhere north of Missouri's southern border.

This was called "The Missouri Compromise." The land divisions of this compromise pointed out how divided the nation had become on the issue of slavery.

Henry Clay (1777–1852)

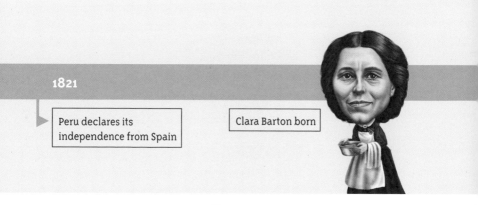

1821

Peru declares its independence from Spain

Clara Barton born

The World's First Steam Railroad

The world's first public railroad revolutionized transportation. Carrying both coal and passengers, the Stockton-Darlington rail line

Ulysses S. Grant born

Brazil gains its independence from Portugal

1822

was built in northeast England in 1825. It helped improve trade and provide jobs. Soon after, railways spread throughout Europe, North America, and the world.

George Stephenson
(1781–1848)

George Stephenson built the Locomotion No. 1, as well as the very first public intercity railway line in the world.

Poem "The Night Before Christmas," or "A Visit from St. Nicholas," by Clement C. Moore is published

Founding Fathers Thomas Jefferson and John Adams both die on July 4

1823   1825   1826

Erie Canal opens, cutting travel time between the Great Lakes and New York City by one third

Charles Darwin's Voyage on the HMS *Beagle* (1831–1836)

In 1831, the crew of the *Beagle* was tasked with a mission to chart the coast of South America. It left England and sailed around the world. During this great adventure, young scientist Charles Darwin studied animals, plants, rocks, and lots of other things. And he took notes on all of it. In the Galapagos Islands, Darwin and the crew saw animals they had never encountered before: marine iguanas, giant tortoises, and many

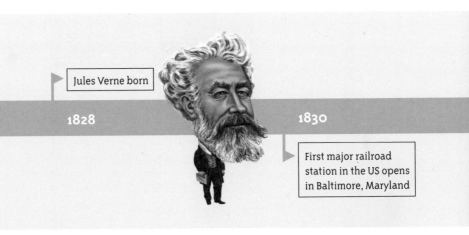

Jules Verne born

1828

1830

First major railroad station in the US opens in Baltimore, Maryland types of birds. Darwin wondered how such an extreme variety of life could ever have occurred.

Years later, he realized that through evolution, many new and different forms of each species were possible. Darwin published his theory of evolution in a book called *On the Origin of Species*. It stated that the world was many millions of years old and that plants and animals change—or evolve—over time.

The initials *HMS* before a ship's name stand for "Her (or His) Majesty's ship" in the British Royal Navy.

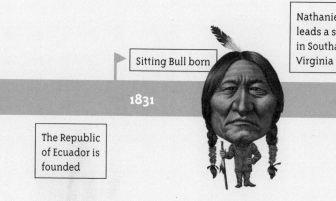

Sitting Bull born

Nathaniel "Nat" Turner leads a slave rebellion in Southampton County, Virginia

1831

The Republic of Ecuador is founded

The Indian Removal Act of 1830

When the United States government wanted to force entire tribes of native people to move west of the Mississippi River, it enacted the Indian Removal Act. As white settlers, fur traders, and pioneers moved westward and into Indian territories, the tribes were forced off their lands.

With their culture nearly destroyed, Eastern Woodlands Indians from the southeastern United States began what is known as the Trail of Tears— a journey to the Cherokee Nation Reservation in

Lewis Carroll born

1832

1835

Danish author Hans Christian Andersen publishes his first book of fairy tales

Oklahoma. Although the Trail of Tears lasted about two months, various battles between the United States and its native peoples lasted for over one hundred years.

CHEROKEE NATION RESERVATION

CHICKASAW

CHEROKEE

CREEK

CHOCTAW

Atlantic Ocean

SEMINOLE

EASTERN WOODLANDS INDIANS TRAIL OF TEARS

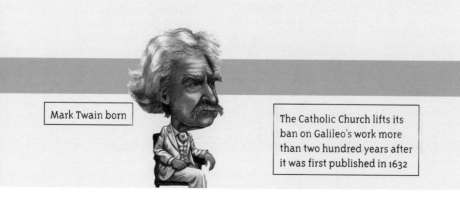

Mark Twain born

The Catholic Church lifts its ban on Galileo's work more than two hundred years after it was first published in 1632

The Opium War

When Britain refused to stop bringing illegal opium—an addictive drug—from India into Chinese ports, China looked for a way to fight back. In 1839, the Chinese destroyed twenty thousand chests of opium, which began the Opium War. The British used the island of Hong Kong as a base during the war. The Royal Navy's warships ravaged Chinese forts. In 1842, the British won the war and the territory of Hong Kong. The Treaty of Nanking officially made Hong Kong a Crown colony of Queen Victoria.

Milton Bradley born

1836

The Battle of the Alamo, one of the key battles of the Mexican-American War

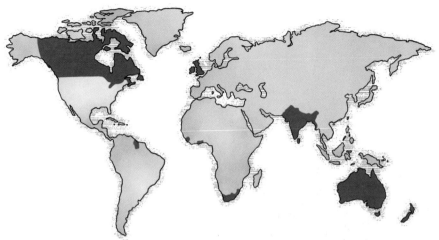

BRITISH EMPIRE 1850

 It wasn't until July 1, 1997, that the British finally transferred their control over Hong Kong back to China. Many people think of this date as marking the end of the British Empire.

1840

Claude Monet born

World's first postage stamp is issued in Britain

The Exploration of Africa

Dr. David Livingstone
(1813–1873)

Dr. David Livingstone was a Scottish missionary from London who opposed the slave trade. In 1841, he traveled to eastern Africa. He spent the next thirty years exploring, and eventually he became the first European to cross the entire continent.

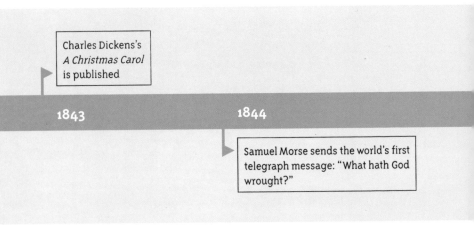

Charles Dickens's
A Christmas Carol
is published

1843

1844

Samuel Morse sends the world's first telegraph message: "What hath God wrought?"

Throughout his time in Africa, Livingstone sent letters to friends and family, detailing his amazing journey.

By the late 1870s, other European nations had become very interested in establishing settlements in Africa. Belgium, Germany, Spain, Great Britain, Italy, France, and Portugal all wanted African colonies of their own—and the wealth that would come from their gold and silver mines. This land grab is known as the "Scramble for Africa."

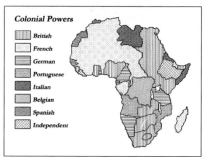

Colonial Powers
- British
- French
- German
- Portuguese
- Italian
- Belgian
- Spanish
- Independent

The Irish Potato Famine begins, eventually leading to one million deaths and two million Irish refugees fleeing their homeland

1845

1847

Thomas Alva Edison born

The California Gold Rush (1848–1855)

John Sutter Sr. (1803–1880)

John Sutter founded a trading fort near the Sacramento River. In 1848, a carpenter named James Marshall who was working for Sutter found gold while building a sawmill at the site. Word of Marshall's discovery spread quickly. Crowds of people poured into the area.

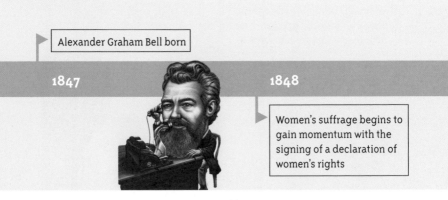

Alexander Graham Bell born

1847

1848

Women's suffrage begins to gain momentum with the signing of a declaration of women's rights

Sutter's son, John Jr., hurried to build a new town for the population boom and named it Sacramento.

In less than a decade, nearly three hundred thousand people arrived in the California Territory of the United States, hoping to find gold. The peak boom was during the year 1849, so the gold miners were nicknamed "forty-niners." Many people were willing to make the overland journey westward in the hope of striking it rich. But of those who did, very few made their fortunes.

More than 750,000 pounds of gold were extracted during the California Gold Rush

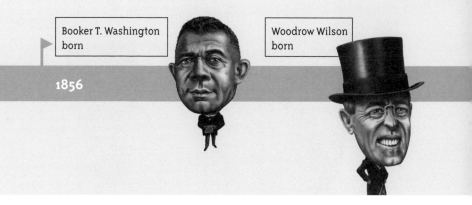

Booker T. Washington born

Woodrow Wilson born

1856

The Underground Railroad

By the mid-1800s, America had become even more divided on the issue of slavery. Abolitionists—those who believed that slavery should be illegal in all of the states—worked with former slaves and free Black people to organize a way to help enslaved people escape to northern "free" states. The Underground Railroad was a system of routes and secret hiding places for those who ran away in search of freedom.

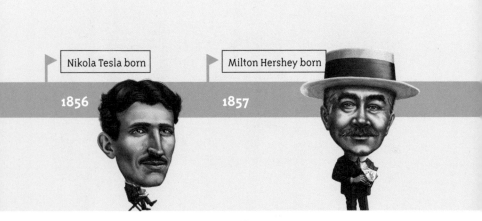

Nikola Tesla born

1856

Milton Hershey born

1857

Harriet Tubman (c. 1820–1913)

Harriet Tubman was an enslaved person who escaped and helped rescue others using the route of the Underground Railroad network. She knew how to use the North Star, near the Big Dipper in the night sky, as a guiding light that showed the way north to freedom. Harriet was also a nurse and a spy for the US Army during the Civil War.

South Carolina Secedes from the Union

Abraham Lincoln won the US presidential election of 1860. He believed that slavery should be abolished in the US territories and not be allowed to expand beyond the states where it was legal. This made many Southerners nervous. They feared that Lincoln's ideas would be very bad for their businesses—like cotton and tobacco farming—that relied so heavily on the unpaid labor of enslaved people.

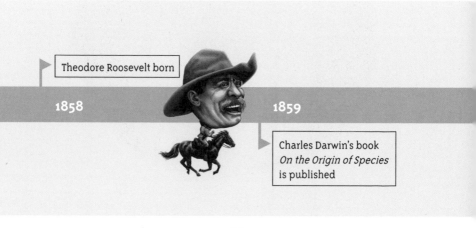

Theodore Roosevelt born

1858

1859

Charles Darwin's book
On the Origin of Species
is published

In December 1860, less than three months before Lincoln's inauguration, South Carolina seceded—or left—the United States. The state legislators there felt that they had to protect South Carolina citizens' "right" to own enslaved people. Other states, including Texas, Louisiana, Mississippi, Alabama, Florida, and Georgia, followed South Carolina and seceded as well. These states established the Confederate States of America on February 4, 1861.

Annie Oakley born

1860

Abraham Lincoln is elected president of the United States

The US Civil War (1861–1865)

When the Confederate States of America (the Confederacy) attacked Fort Sumter, South Carolina, on April 12, 1861, it ignited a long and violent conflict that resulted in nearly two million deaths. The US Civil War lasted for four long years. During that time, the Union army of the North fought the Confederate army of the South in over two hundred bloody battles and skirmishes. Union general Ulysses S. Grant knew he would have to destroy factories and railroads

George Washington Carver born

1861

1862

Mexicans defeat Emperor Maximilian's troops at the Battle of Puebla, May 5, 1862, commemorated today as Cinco de Mayo

to hurt the Southern army's resources and defeat the Confederacy. Southern general Robert E. Lee finally did surrender at Appomattox Court House in Virginia on April 9, 1865.

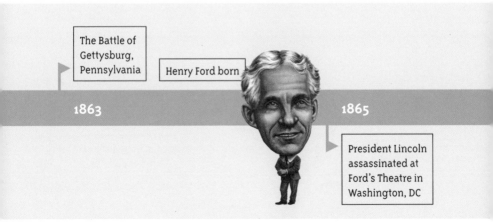

The Battle of Gettysburg, Pennsylvania

Henry Ford born

1863

1865

President Lincoln assassinated at Ford's Theatre in Washington, DC

The Aftermath of Slavery

When President Lincoln signed the Emancipation Proclamation on January 1, 1863, he changed the legal status of three million enslaved people from slave to free. But that did not mean that they could simply walk away from the plantations they lived and worked on.

The Civil War had destroyed much Southern wealth. Most banks were bankrupt, and freed slaves meant the loss of unpaid labor. The northern and western areas of the United States began to

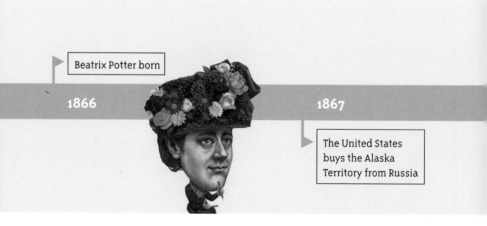

Beatrix Potter born

1866

1867

The United States buys the Alaska Territory from Russia

grow richer as the South grew even poorer. Many formerly enslaved people stayed and worked in the same fields they had always labored in, though for very little pay.

The Thirteenth Amendment to the US Constitution officially ended slavery in all states for good in 1865.

ABOLISHING SLAVERY.

Laura Ingalls Wilder born

Austro-Hungarian Empire forms

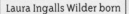

The Industrial Revolution at Its Peak

Between about 1760 and 1860, many inventions helped transform Great Britain into the first industrial power in the world. Water-powered mills turned into the first factories. And the steam locomotive helped expand railway shipping and transportation. Iron, coal, and rivers were the raw ingredients necessary to produce more goods at a much quicker pace than ever before. Men, women, and children all went to work in factories. More factories contributed to the fast-paced growth of cities.

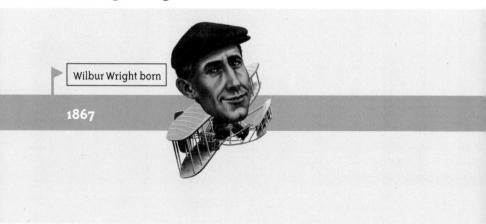

Wilbur Wright born

1867

The Lowell Mill Girls

One of the biggest factory complexes in America was the group of textile mills that wove fabric in Lowell, Massachusetts. Young women worked seventy-three hours a week, from 5:00 a.m. until 7:00 p.m. every day. They worked and ate together, living in boardinghouses that had been built by the factory owners. By 1840, over eight thousand women were employed at the mills. And by 1848, Lowell was the largest industrial center in America, producing fifty thousand *miles* of cotton cloth each year!

The Suez Canal

The first ship sailed through the Suez Canal on November 17, 1869. The canal, built in Egypt by an international team of engineers, connected the Mediterranean Sea and the Red Sea for the first time in history.

The Suez Canal is now the shortest route between Europe and Asia. Before its construction, ships had to sail all the way around the southern tip of Africa—called the Cape of Good Hope—to reach India, China, and Southeast Asia.

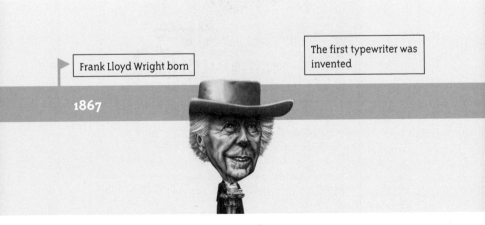

Frank Lloyd Wright born

The first typewriter was invented

1867

Marie Curie born

The First Transcontinental Railroad

It took six years for workers to complete the rail lines that connect the East and West Coasts of the United States. The Central Pacific Railroad started in California. And the Union Pacific Railroad began from rail lines in Iowa.

The two teams met on May 10, 1869, in Promontory, Utah. A golden spike (a large railroad nail) was driven into the tracks during a ceremony that celebrated the enormous importance of

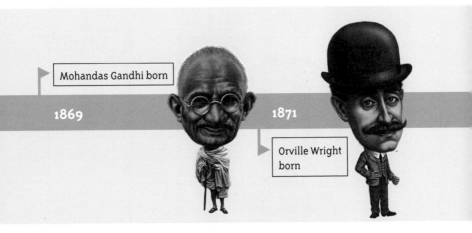

Mohandas Gandhi born

1869

1871

Orville Wright born

uniting the country by rail. People—and a huge variety of goods—could now move across the country much quicker, opening up the culture and the economy of the United States in new and dramatic ways.

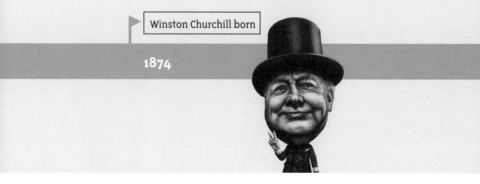

Winston Churchill born

1874

The Wizard of Menlo Park

In 1876, the great American inventor Thomas Alva Edison opened the world's first industrial research laboratory in Menlo Park, New Jersey. In 1878, he filed his patent for the "improvement in electric lights." Edison went on to perfect the incandescent lightbulb and patent more than one thousand other inventions. Among them:

- movie camera
- phonographic cylinder
- carbon microphone

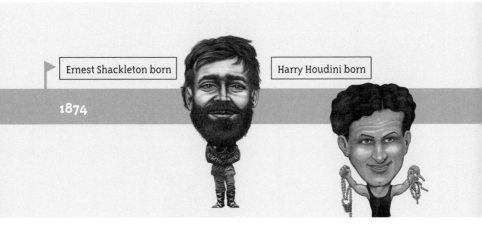

Ernest Shackleton born

Harry Houdini born

1874

- vacuum diode
- vitascope (an early film projector)
- mimeograph (an early copy machine)
- alkaline storage battery
- electric lamp
- autographic printer
- improvements to the telephone
- film
- electric vote recorder
- stencil pen
- vacuum pump improvements

1876

| Alexander Graham Bell invents the telephone | The United States celebrates its centennial—its 100th birthday | Britain's Queen Victoria takes the title "Empress of India" |

83

The Zulu War, South Africa

The Zulu Nation in South Africa had been established by the warrior chief Shaka in the early 1800s.

During the colonization of the African continent by Europeans, the British fought the Zulu Kingdom from January to July 1879. The British won, and the Zulu king was captured. The Zulus' control of

Albert Einstein born

1879

the region ended. Zululand—all the land once controlled by the Zulu Nation—was divided into thirteen new areas with thirteen new chiefs who were all under British control.

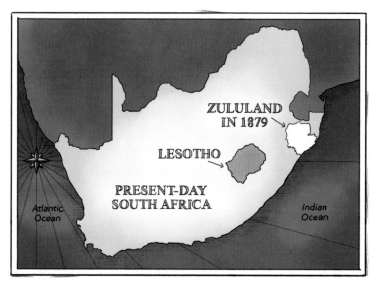

ZULULAND
IN 1879

LESOTHO

PRESENT-DAY
SOUTH AFRICA

Atlantic
Ocean

Indian
Ocean

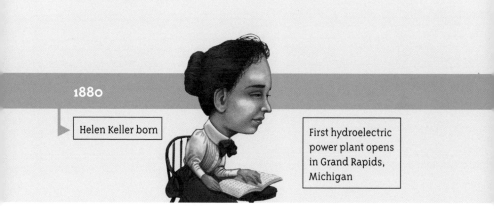

1880

Helen Keller born

First hydroelectric
power plant opens
in Grand Rapids,
Michigan

The Victorian Era

Queen Victoria ruled Great Britain and the British Empire from 1837 until her death in 1901—a very long time! She had nine children and forty grandchildren!

Her reign, known as the Victorian Era, was a prosperous one for her country. During her time as queen, the British Empire expanded to colonies in Africa, Asia, the Americas, and Australia. The world was changing rapidly with huge improvements in manufacturing, medicine, and engineering.

Sitting Bull is captured as a prisoner of war

Clara Barton establishes the American Red Cross

1881

Queen Victoria was the first person to be pictured on a postage stamp, the first person to send a telegraph from one continent to another, and the first monarch to be photographed!

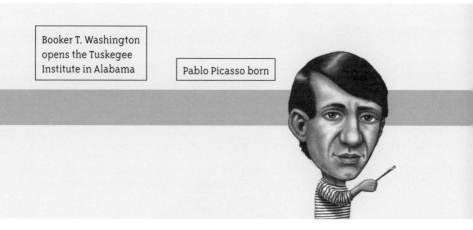

Booker T. Washington opens the Tuskegee Institute in Alabama

Pablo Picasso born

The Orient Express

During the great age of steam, people were able to travel longer distances much more

Franklin Roosevelt born

1882

easily. The first route of the Orient Express traveled an international route from Paris, France, to Istanbul (then Constantinople), Turkey, in 1883. (The journey took about eighty hours.) But this was no cargo train! The "lightning luxury train" was for passengers and had fancy sleeping cars, separate baggage cars, and a restaurant car that specialized in fine dining. At a time when travel could still be a bit rough and sometimes dangerous, the Orient Express symbolized only the best of the best!

The menu on board the very first Orient Express train included oysters, fish in green sauce, beef with potatoes, and chocolate pudding.

Gold is discovered in Witwatersrand, South Africa

1884

1886

Eleanor Roosevelt born

The Paris Exhibition of 1889

This historic world's fair, held in Paris from May through October 1889, was an international exhibition that celebrated the one hundredth anniversary of the storming of the Bastille prison at the start of the French Revolution. People came from all over the world to showcase their talents and to visit. American Buffalo Bill invited sharpshooter Annie Oakley to perform at his Wild West Show—a sellout attraction of the exposition.

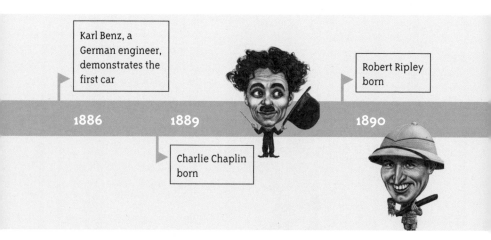

Karl Benz, a German engineer, demonstrates the first car

1886

1889

Charlie Chaplin born

Robert Ripley born

1890

The Eiffel Tower

The Eiffel Tower, engineered and built by Gustave Eiffel, was the main attraction at the Paris Exhibition. Its legs served as the entryway to the fair. At 984 feet tall, it was the world's tallest building until 1930.

The Massacre at Wounded Knee

In the spring of 1889, the US government opened up lands that had previously been set aside as Indian Territory to settlers moving westward. This area, in what is now Oklahoma, was the last place in the United States that was still considered to be "unsettled" by white pioneers. The government was giving the green light to miners and ranchers to move in and settle the last of this territory. Many Native Americans were displaced. They longed for a more peaceful

J. R. R. Tolkien born

1892

1893

New Zealand becomes the first country in the world to allow women the right to vote

and prosperous time and a chance to regain their land.

In December 1890, when the Sioux gathered on the Pine Ridge Indian Reservation in South Dakota to hold a ghost dance ceremony, US troops attacked and killed hundreds of the tribe near  Wounded Knee Creek. The massacre at Wounded Knee was the last major battle between the US government and its indigenous people.

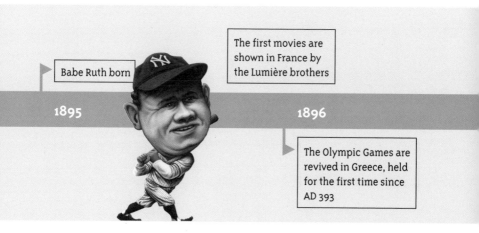

Babe Ruth born

1895

The first movies are shown in France by the Lumière brothers

1896

The Olympic Games are revived in Greece, held for the first time since AD 393

93

The Spanish-American War

In 1895, José Martí began the fight for Cuban independence from Spain. Some Americans thought that the island of Cuba, which is very close to Florida, would be lost as a trade partner if Spain was victorious. In 1898, the US Congress declared war on Spain and the Spanish-American War had begun. On December 10 of that year, the US and Spain signed the Treaty of Paris, ending the war. Spain gave up its colonies of Puerto Rico, Guam, and the Philippines to the US. Cuba became an independent nation.

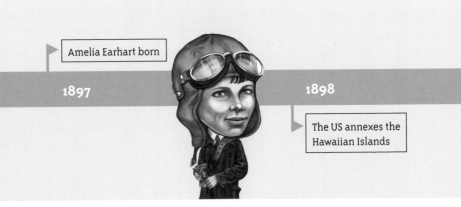

Amelia Earhart born

1897

1898

The US annexes the Hawaiian Islands

Teddy Roosevelt's Rough Riders

During the Spanish-American War, Theodore Roosevelt organized a group of cavalry volunteers who called themselves the Rough Riders. This regiment of ranchers, cowboys, miners, and college students were excellent horsemen who helped win the Battle of San Juan Hill in Cuba on July 1, 1898.

Nikola Tesla Invents the Twentieth Century

The modern era was ushered in at the dawn of the twentieth century. New technologies were being developed and adopted rapidly across the globe.

Nikola Tesla (1856–1943) was a Serbian American engineer and inventor who made major contributions to the way we use electricity. He refined the power grid and the use of AC current. He was ahead of his time with ideas about remote

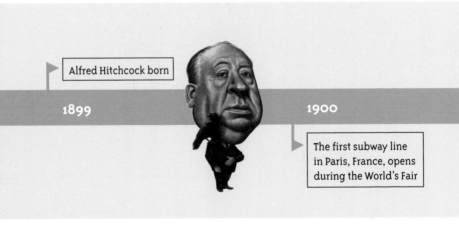

Alfred Hitchcock born

1899

1900

The first subway line in Paris, France, opens during the World's Fair control and wireless communications. Tesla is widely considered to be the great genius who made much of twentieth-century technology possible.

Scientists who study predictions about the future and look for ways to make those ideas a reality in the present are known as futurists. Nikola Tesla is one of the most famous examples of a futurist.

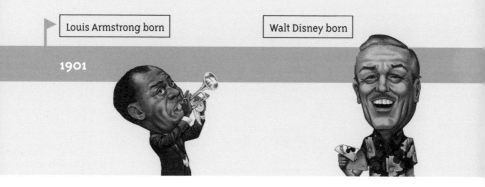

Louis Armstrong born

Walt Disney born

1901

Flight!

The Wright Flyer made the first powered, controlled flight with a pilot off the sand dunes of Kitty Hawk, North Carolina, in 1903. Built by brothers Orville and Wilbur Wright, the Wright Flyer was the world's first successful airplane. On December 17, Orville Wright flew 120 feet in twelve seconds. Later that same day, Wilbur completed an 852-foot flight in just under a minute.

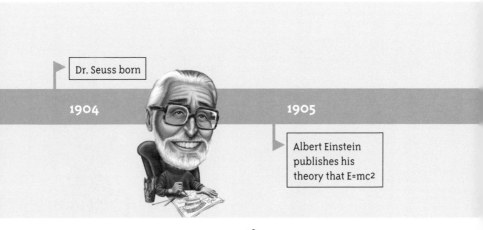

Dr. Seuss born

1904

1905

Albert Einstein publishes his theory that E=mc2

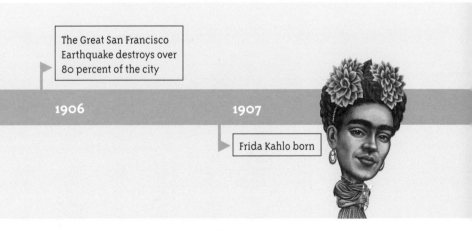

The Great San Francisco
Earthquake destroys over
80 percent of the city

1906

1907

Frida Kahlo born

Beep! Beep!

Henry Ford produced the first Model T car in 1908. Known as the Tin Lizzie, Ford's car changed the way Americans lived, worked, and traveled.

By 1913, Ford had perfected the assembly line production system, which produced cars more quickly and made them more affordable for the public. The assembly line reduced the time it took to build a car from twelve hours to just two and a half. In 1916, the cars began selling for $345— less than half of their original price of $850.

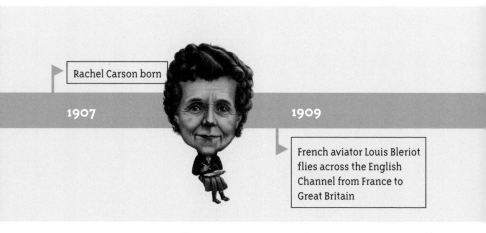

Rachel Carson born

1907

1909

French aviator Louis Bleriot flies across the English Channel from France to Great Britain

Between 1913 and 1927, Ford's American assembly lines produced more than fifteen million Model Ts!

1910

Jacques Cousteau born

The Mexican Revolution begins

Roald Amundsen Becomes the First Person to Reach the South Pole

When Norwegian Roald Amundsen found out that Robert Perry had beat him to the North Pole, he turned around and headed south! Amundsen and his crew reached the South Pole in December 1911, winning the race one month ahead of Britain's Robert Scott. Amundsen and Scott's race to the pole had been followed closely by people all around the world. But Amundsen

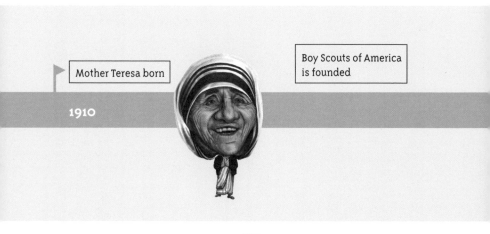

Mother Teresa born

Boy Scouts of America is founded

1910

was a more experienced explorer who was better prepared and more accustomed to polar conditions. Scott and the last of his crew froze to death on the return trip home, only eleven miles from their One Ton supply depot.

Roald Amundsen (1872–1928)

1911

Lucille Ball born

Ronald Reagan born

The Sinking of the *Titanic*

The RMS (royal mail ship) *Titanic* was the heaviest and finest ship ever built. In April 1912, on its very first voyage, the ship sped across the Atlantic Ocean from England to New York. It was carrying around 2,200 people, both passengers and crew.

At about 11:40 p.m. on the clear and bitterly cold night of April 14, the ship's lookout spotted an iceberg. But it was too late to stop or turn. The mightiest ship of the White Star Line was

Chuck Jones born

Julia Child born

1912

damaged and taking on water fast. Within two hours, it began sinking. And by 2:20 a.m. on the morning of April 15, the *Titanic* slipped into the ocean.

Over half of the people on board—1,503 in total—died during the disaster. But the *Titanic* lives on, in movies, plays, television shows, and books, as the most famous shipwreck in history.

1913

Rosa Parks born

Jesse Owens born

World War I (1914–1918)

There were many causes that contributed to World War I, such as countries wanting to prove their patriotism and might. But the single event that triggered the start of the war was the assassination of Archduke Franz Ferdinand of Austria-Hungary and his wife, Sophie, on June 28, 1914. They were killed by a young Bosnian-Serb man while touring Bosnia.

Austria-Hungary quickly declared war on Serbia, and alliances throughout Europe were formed. When Germany invaded France, World

The Panama Canal, linking the Atlantic and Pacific Oceans, is completed

1914

1915

First air battles, the dogfights of World War I

War I (also called the Great War) was underway. The war was fought by these two sides:

The Central Powers	*The Allied Powers*
Austria-Hungary	Serbia
Germany	Russia
The Ottoman Empire	France
Bulgaria	Great Britain
	Belgium
	and later, the
	United States,
	Japan, and Italy
	and others

Roald Dahl born

First battle tanks
used by the British
in World War I

1916

The End of the Great War

In April 1917, the United States declared war on Germany, entering World War I. After the Russian government was overthrown and both German and Austrian leaders gave up their thrones, Germany and the Allied powers signed the Treaty of Versailles. World War I was officially over.

The main terms of the Treaty of Versailles, signed on June 28, 1919:

Explorer Ernest Shackleton and his team are rescued from Elephant Island, off the coast of Antarctica

National Parks Service established by US Congress

1916

- Germany had to accept sole responsibility for the war.
- Germany's army was reduced to 100,000 soldiers.
- Germany had to pay other countries that it had damaged during the war.
- Germany had to return the Alsace-Lorraine region to France.

EXTRA | THE EVENING WORLD | HOME EDITION

TREATY SIGNED; WAR OVER

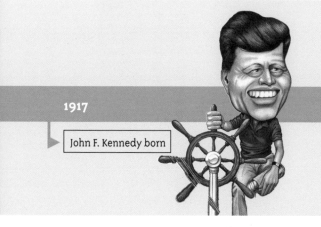

1917

John F. Kennedy born

The Russian Revolution (1917)

During World War I, Russia struggled with many casualties and food shortages. Life was difficult and the Russian people were making every effort to survive. After Czar Nicholas II was forced to step down in 1917, Vladimir Lenin took control of the Russian government and set up the communist system—the state would control everything. Members of Lenin's revolutionary group were called the Bolsheviks. They later became the Communist Party.

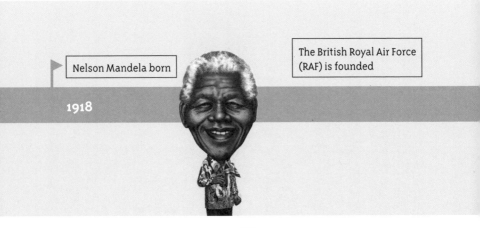

Nelson Mandela born

The British Royal Air Force (RAF) is founded

1918

Vladimir Lenin (1870–1924)

After World War I ended, Russia merged with other Soviet republics to form the USSR (the Union of Soviet Socialist Republics, also known as the Soviet Union) in 1922.

1919

Jackie Robinson born

Pete Seeger born

The Discovery of King Tut's Tomb

English archaeologist Howard Carter located King Tut's tomb in Egypt in November 1922. He had been digging in the Valley of the Kings on the western bank of the Nile River. The expedition had been paid for by George Herbert, the fifth Earl of Carnarvon. And Carter waited two full weeks for Lord Carnarvon to arrive from England before opening the door of the burial chamber at the end of a stone stairway.

Once they entered the tomb, Carter and

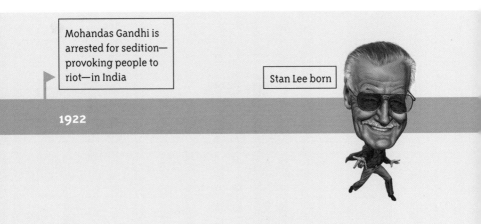

Mohandas Gandhi is arrested for sedition—provoking people to riot—in India

Stan Lee born

1922

112

his crew found statues, gold, chariots, a throne, vases, and many other beautiful ancient Egyptian treasures. Beyond another door lay the undisturbed mummy of King Tutankhamen, the boy king of Egypt who had been born around 1341 BCE.

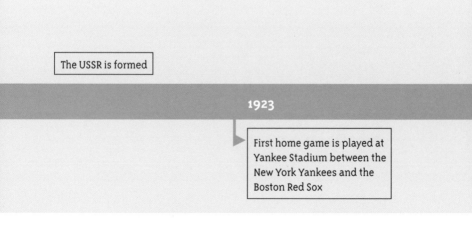

The USSR is formed

1923

First home game is played at Yankee Stadium between the New York Yankees and the Boston Red Sox

The Jazz Age

As transportation and communication became easier and more affordable, American culture was forever changed. The American economy was improving and industries were modernizing quickly. During the decade of the 1920s—also called the Roaring Twenties— people had shorter work days, shorter work weeks, and more time for fun—like dancing the Charleston and the Jitterbug. Radio, film, and American pastimes like baseball grew into major businesses.

St. Petersburg, Russia, renamed Leningrad

US citizenship granted to all Native Americans

1924

Jazz

Jazz, which originated in New Orleans and spread north to cities like Chicago and New York, is a combination of African American and European music that transformed into a truly unique American music. Trumpeter Louis Armstrong was a trailblazing pioneer of jazz music during the 1920s and beyond.

The Harlem Renaissance

During and after World War I, many African Americans moved from the southern United States to the North in what was known as the Great Migration. Seeking work in larger cities with numerous factories, they formed thriving neighborhoods like the one called Harlem in New York City.

The Harlem Renaissance of the 1920s was an exciting movement of artists, writers, and musicians who were influenced by the jazz and

Maria Tallchief born

1925

blues of the South but were also energized by the bustle of city life. Poet Langston Hughes, composer and musician Duke Ellington, and author Zora Neale Hurston are just a few of the famous names to emerge during the Harlem Renaissance.

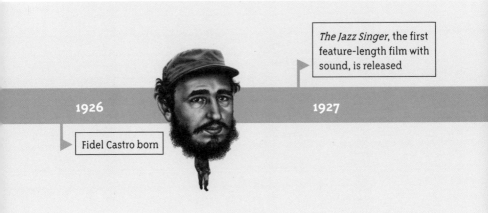

1926

Fidel Castro born

1927

The Jazz Singer, the first feature-length film with sound, is released

Mount Rushmore

The US government had seized the Black Hills of South Dakota from the Lakota tribe after the Great Sioux War of 1876. Fifty years later, historian Doane Robinson thought of carving the mountain to increase tourism to the area. In 1924, sculptor Gutzon Borglum took on the huge task of carving. With the help of his son, Lincoln, he began creating sixty-foot sculptures of four US presidents: George Washington, Thomas Jefferson, Theodore Roosevelt, and Abraham Lincoln. The blasting and carving lasted from 1927 until 1941, when the monument was finally completed.

Cesar Chavez born

Coretta Scott King born

1927

But Who Was Rushmore?

New York City lawyer Charles E. Rushmore was sent to South Dakota in 1884 to check legal property titles to land in the Black Hills region. When he asked what the name of the mountain was, a local guide told him that it "never had a name. But from now on, we'll call it 'Rushmore.'"

Stalin's Five-Year Plan

After Vladimir Lenin's death in 1924, the Communist Party of the USSR was open to new leadership. A government official named Joseph Stalin stepped in and took control with his Five-Year Plan in 1928.

Stalin wanted to transform the USSR from a nation of farms to a nation of factories, producing military equipment and heavy machinery. The government controlled the farmlands *and* the factories. But the Soviet people were suffering from low pay and horrible living conditions.

Maya Angelou born

1928

Maurice Sendak born

Joseph Stalin (1878–1953)

Anyone who disagreed with Stalin was killed or sent to labor camps in the cold and desolate region of Siberia and forced to do difficult work in mines and forests there. Stalin's Five-Year Plan was not successful.

Amelia Earhart is the first woman to fly across the Atlantic Ocean

Andy Warhol born

The Three Stooges, Moe, Larry, and Shemp, begin performing together

Black Tuesday

As the US economy grew and expanded throughout the 1920s, business, industry, and farms produced and sold more goods than ever before. For the first time, many ordinary citizens (people who did not work for banks, or investment firms, or in the nation's financial capital of Wall Street in New York City) bought stocks—or small shares—in these booming businesses. They invested their savings in the hope of one day sharing in the profits.

On October 29, 1929—which came to be

Martin Luther King Jr. born

The First Academy Awards are held in Hollywood, California

1929

known as Black Tuesday—the value of these shares suddenly dropped, and the US stock market "crashed" when the stocks became worthless. Many people lost their entire life's savings. Businesses across the country had to close or reduce their size, laying off workers. Unemployment became a major issue. Even those who still had jobs could no longer afford to spend money as they once had. The Great Depression was looming.

Anne Frank born

The Great Depression (1929–1939)

The stock market crash of Black Tuesday in 1929 had a major impact on the US economy:

- Twenty thousand companies were bankrupt
- More than 1,600 banks were bankrupt
- Twelve million people were out of work
- One in every twenty farmers was evicted because they could no longer pay the mortgages—the bank loans—on their farms

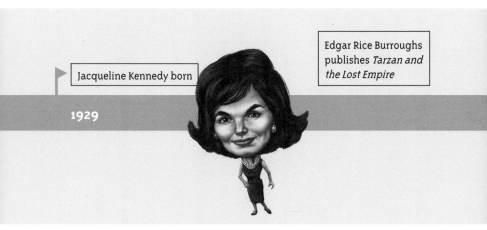

Jacqueline Kennedy born

Edgar Rice Burroughs publishes *Tarzan and the Lost Empire*

1929

Herbert Hoover (1874–1964)

The US president—Herbert Hoover—was a Republican. He believed that it was not the responsibility of the government to help individuals or to provide relief. In 1932, Hoover said, "Prosperity is just around the corner." But he was very wrong about that.

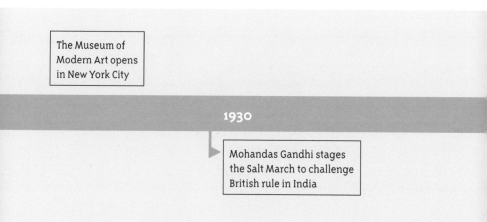

The Museum of Modern Art opens in New York City

1930

Mohandas Gandhi stages the Salt March to challenge British rule in India

FDR's New Deal

Franklin Delano Roosevelt (1882–1945)

Franklin D. Roosevelt (FDR), a Democrat, was elected president in 1932. He quickly enacted a program called the New Deal to help the

Neil Armstrong born

1930

US economy recover. This "deal" included help for farmers and unemployed people. It created new jobs building roads, bridges, and airports.

FDR designed a second New Deal in 1935, establishing the Works Progress Administration to create over three million more new jobs. The second "deal" also included the Social Security Act, which created a national system that US workers contribute to in order to save money for their retirement.

The Works Progress Administration (WPA) created jobs not only for engineers and construction workers but also for thousands of artists. WPA projects created more than 2,500 murals and 17,744 sculptures, which adorned public buildings across the country.

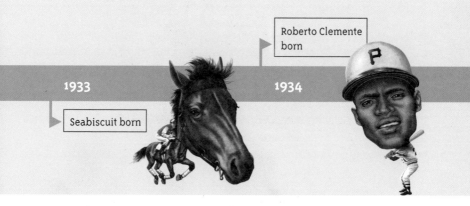

Roberto Clemente born

1933

1934

Seabiscuit born

Birth of the Comic Book

In 1933, Eastern Color Printing published *Famous Funnies* #1, considered to be the first American comic book. It featured comics, games, puzzles, and magic tricks.

The Sultan of Swat

In 1927, Babe Ruth signed a contract with the New York Yankees worth $70,000 per year for three years. That year, he hit sixty home runs as a Yankee. "The Bambino"—as he was known—went on to become the greatest baseball player of all time.

On July 13, 1934, he hit his 700th home run.

Babe Ruth's number, 3, was retired by the Yankees on June 13, 1948, during his final appearance at Yankee Stadium, which had become known as "The House That Ruth Built."

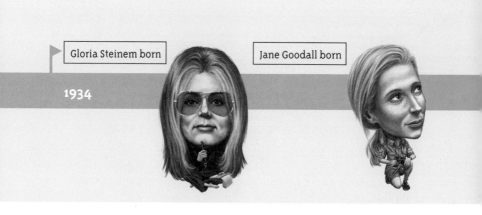

Gloria Steinem born

Jane Goodall born

1934

The 1936 Berlin Olympics and the Fastest Runner in the World

The Nazi Party, led by Adolf Hitler, had risen to power in Germany three years before the Berlin Olympics of 1936. Hitler hoped that the Olympic Games would prove his belief that white people—and especially white German people—were the best race on earth. His racist ideas created tension among the athletes, and some countries threatened to boycott the games.

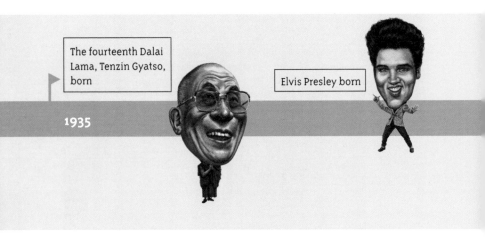

The fourteenth Dalai Lama, Tenzin Gyatso, born

Elvis Presley born

1935

African American runner Jesse Owens stunned Hitler and the world by winning four gold medals for the United States. He was the most successful athlete to compete in Berlin and broke or equaled nine Olympic records. He even set three new world records! Jesse Owens—a Black man—was the fastest man in the world.

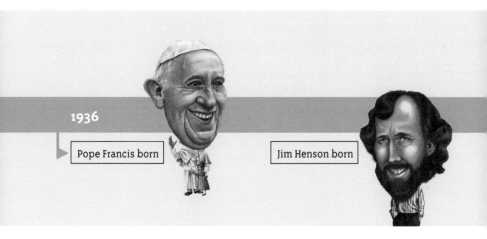

1936

Pope Francis born

Jim Henson born

Germany Invades Poland

Adolf Hitler (1889–1945)

Adolf Hitler and the Nazi Party wanted to dominate Europe by creating an empire they called the Third Reich. (*Reich* is the German word for "empire.") Hitler formed alliances with Italy (and later Japan) and began to move

Pablo Picasso completes one of his most famous paintings, *Guernica*, as an antiwar statement after the Nazi Party bombs the Spanish town of Guernica

Amelia Earhart disappears over the Pacific Ocean

1937

his armies into Czechoslovakia. In September 1939, Hitler invaded Poland.

Great Britain and France saw what an enormous, serious threat Hitler had become and declared war on Germany. World War II had begun.

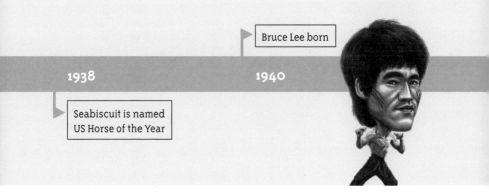

Seabiscuit is named US Horse of the Year

1938

Bruce Lee born

1940

World War II

The United States entered World War II on December 7, 1941, after the Japanese bombed the US naval base at Pearl Harbor, Hawaii. The two opposing sides of the war were:

The Axis Powers	*The Allied Powers*
Germany	Great Britain
Italy	France
Japan	USSR
	United States
	China

Bob Dylan born

1941

The Holocaust

In countries occupied by the Nazis, Jewish people were forced into districts called ghettos. In 1942, Hitler ordered the Jews to be transported from the ghettos and killed. He called it the final solution. Eleven million people died in the Holocaust, a word that means "sacrifice by fire." They labored in work camps and were starved to death, killed in gas chambers, and buried in mass graves. Six million Jews died, along with five million people from groups that included those with disabilities, homosexuals, Catholics, and anyone who opposed the Nazi Party.

1942

Muhammad Ali born

Bing Crosby records the song "White Christmas," now the best-selling single in the world

D-Day

On June 6, 1944, Allied-force warships landed in northern France on Normandy beaches. The Allies soon freed France from German control, and the push to free the rest of Europe from the Axis powers was underway.

George Lucas born

1944

US government establishes the Office of Strategic Services (OSS)—later called the Central Intelligence Agency (CIA)

The DUKW

The Allies' D-Day success was due in part to the six-wheeled trucks that carried both supplies and troops. Commonly called "ducks," these American-built vehicles were amphibious—they could be used on both land (as trucks) and in water (as boats).

Dropping the
Atomic Bombs

The weapons of World War II were bigger and deadlier than in any previous war. On August 6, 1945, an American plane dropped a single atomic bomb on the city of Hiroshima, Japan, killing 66,000 people instantly and 140,000 by year's end.

Japan refused to surrender, and three days later the United States dropped a second bomb on the town of Nagasaki, killing between 60,000 and 80,000 more Japanese people.

Bob Marley born

1945

On August 14, 1945, Japan surrendered. The surrender documents were signed on September 2, and World War II officially came to an end.

1946

Dolly Parton born

Steven Spielberg born

The Establishment of the United Nations

At the end of World War II, fifty-one countries signed a charter to create a world community of independent nations. This community is called the United Nations (UN). It is committed to

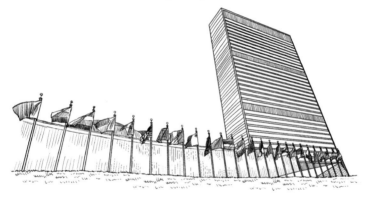

The first of the Dead Sea Scrolls, which contained partial manuscripts of the Old Testament of the Bible, are found in caves along the West Bank of the Jordan River

Elton John born

1947

protecting international peace and taking action against countries that threaten war.

The UN currently has 193 member nations that have equal representation in the UN General Assembly. It is based in New York City.

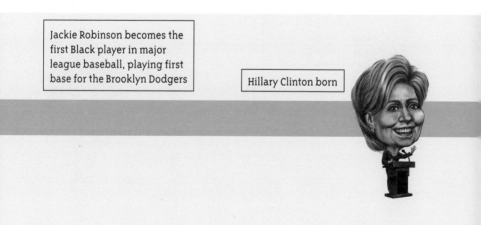

Jackie Robinson becomes the first Black player in major league baseball, playing first base for the Brooklyn Dodgers

Hillary Clinton born

India Gains Independence from Great Britain

After decades of nonviolent resistance, protests, and marches, the Indian people finally gained their independence from British rule in 1947. Mohandas Gandhi led the cause by peaceful example. He is often called Mahatma, meaning "great soul."

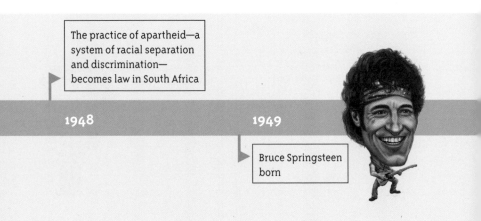

The practice of apartheid—a system of racial separation and discrimination—becomes law in South Africa

1948

1949

Bruce Springsteen born

Creation of the State of Israel

In 1947, the United Nations declared that part of the country of Palestine—then controlled by the British—be made a Jewish state as a homeland for the Jewish people. And in 1948, Israel was officially formed. The Muslim Arabs who lived in Palestine (the Gaza Strip and the West Bank), as well as the neighboring Arab countries, were not happy about the UN's decision. The conflict between Palestine and Israel continues to this day.

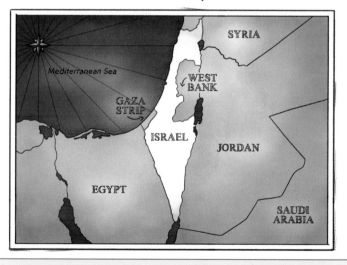

The Cold War

After World War II, tensions grew between the United States and Western Europe on one side and the USSR and Eastern Europe on the other. In 1949, Germany was divided into two countries: West Germany (controlled by the Allies) and East Germany (controlled by the USSR). The capital itself, the city of Berlin, was divided by a wall that came to symbolize the division between the two opposing sides.

The two most influential countries to emerge from World War II were the United States and

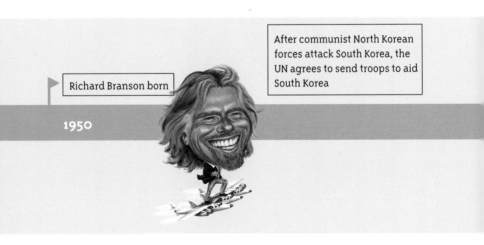

Richard Branson born

1950

After communist North Korean forces attack South Korea, the UN agrees to send troops to aid South Korea

the USSR. Known as "superpowers," these two sides were not fighting on a battlefield. They were waging a "cold" war over the ideals of communism and democracy. The United States does not believe a government should own and control all factories, farms, and businesses. But communists do. And the communist governments don't allow free elections or freedom of speech, as in a democracy. During the Cold War, the United States believed it had to defend democracy against the spread of communism around the world.

British prime minister Winston Churchill once said: "An iron curtain has descended across the continent." "Iron Curtain" became a common way to refer to the separation of Eastern and Western Europe during the Cold War.

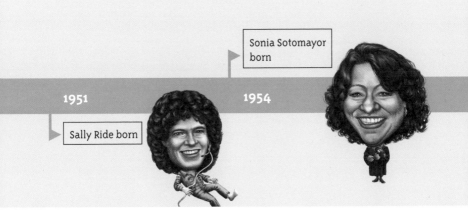

Sonia Sotomayor born

1951

1954

Sally Ride born

The Vietnam War (November 1, 1955– April 30, 1975)

In 1954, the country of Vietnam was divided into the communist North and the anti-communist South. US president Dwight Eisenhower sent money and weapons to support the army of South Vietnam. But the South was plagued by rebel communist forces from the North, called the Vietcong. The army of South Vietnam was losing control of its territory.

In 1955, China and the USSR pledged to

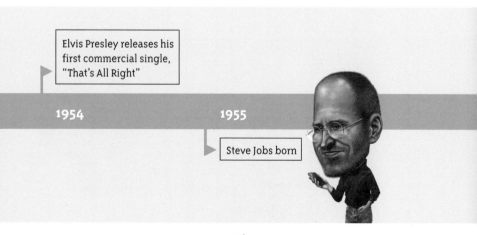

Elvis Presley releases his first commercial single, "That's All Right"

1954

1955

Steve Jobs born

send help to the North Vietnamese. The United States entered the war with the hope of stopping the North Vietnamese army from spreading communism to the South. But the jungles of Southeast Asia were difficult territory for American troops. Just as in the Korean War from 1950 to 1953, the United States failed to defeat the Northern communists.

Bill Gates born

Rosa Parks is arrested in Montgomery, Alabama, after refusing to give up her seat on the bus to a white passenger

The Little Rock Nine

Since the end of the US Civil War, racist "Jim Crow" laws had kept white and Black Americans separated from one another in public life—from drinking fountains to buses to schools. The US Supreme Court's 1896 decision permitted segregation to continue, as long as the facilities were "separate but equal." But the public schools attended by Black students were often inferior in many ways to the white schools. So in 1954, the Supreme Court ruled that public schools had to integrate—to allow both Black and white students

The Southern Christian Leadership Council is founded with Martin Luther King Jr. as its president

The Anne Frank Foundation is formed in Amsterdam

1957

to attend the same schools.

Segregationists—people who preferred to keep students separated by race—delayed the process of school integration for years after the Supreme Court ruling. In 1957, a judge ordered Little Rock Central High School in Little Rock, Arkansas, to admit nine Black students. But the governor of Arkansas believed in segregation. He used the state's National Guard soldiers to keep the Black students out of the school for three weeks. President Dwight Eisenhower sent federal troops to protect the students—known as the Little Rock Nine—as they entered the school.

The final broadcast of *I Love Lucy* TV show airs

US president Eisenhower signs the Civil Rights Act of 1957 to help protect the voter rights of all citizens

The Space Race

The Soviet Union launched the first man-made satellite, called Sputnik, in 1957. It was the very first object sent into space. Two years later, they launched Luna 2. This propelled the United States and the USSR into a "space race" to see which country would be the first to send humans into space and which would be the first to reach the moon. This race led to the creation and funding of NASA in the United States.

NASA, the National Aeronautics and Space Administration, was founded in 1958. In 1960,

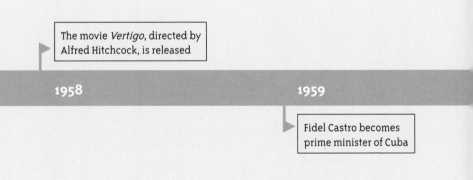

The movie *Vertigo*, directed by Alfred Hitchcock, is released

1958

1959

Fidel Castro becomes prime minister of Cuba

NASA established the Mercury project to test if humans could survive in space. It was determined to have an American reach the moon by the end of the decade. On May 5, 1961, Alan Shepard became the first American to travel into space. He was less than one month behind the Soviet cosmonaut Yuri Gagarin, who made the historic *first* flight on April 12, 1961.

Yuri Gagarin (1934–1968) and Alan Shepard (1923–1998)

The Beatles formed

1960

The Cuban Missile Crisis

In 1959, communist dictator Fidel Castro became the prime minister of Cuba. The island nation of Cuba is only ninety miles from the United States, and the American government was determined to remove him from power, partly because Castro's government had become dependent on the Soviet Union for military and economic support. But the US invasion in 1961—known as the Bay of Pigs Invasion after its Cuban location—was a failure.

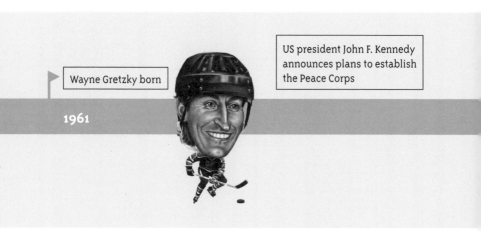

Wayne Gretzky born

US president John F. Kennedy announces plans to establish the Peace Corps

1961

In October 1962, the United States detected Soviet missile sites in Cuba. US president John F. Kennedy ordered a naval blockade to stop Soviet ships from delivering nuclear weapons to the island. The blockade—from October 16 to October 28—succeeded, and the missiles were removed. In turn, the United States agreed not to invade Cuba. The Cuban Missile Crisis was over.

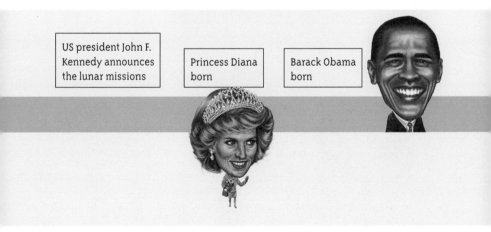

US president John F. Kennedy announces the lunar missions

Princess Diana born

Barack Obama born

The March on Washington for Jobs and Freedom

On August 28, 1963, Reverend Martin Luther King Jr. led a march in Washington, DC. More than 250,000 people from around the United States came to march with him. They arrived to show their support of the civil rights bill that President Kennedy had asked Congress to create two months earlier. The bill supported equal rights for all Americans.

Near the Lincoln Memorial, Reverend King

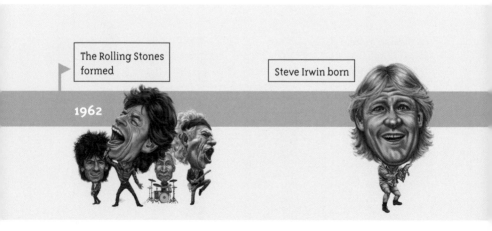

The Rolling Stones formed

Steve Irwin born

1962

spoke about his dream of unity. With his hopeful message of brotherhood and freedom, Martin Luther King Jr. became the voice of the civil rights movement and inspired generations of civil rights activists. The March on Washington was one of the largest political rallies for human rights in US history.

Nelson Mandela is arrested in South Africa

Stan Lee's Spider-Man debuts in Marvel Comics *Amazing Fantasy* #15

The British Invasion

In February 1964, a CBS news reporter, commenting on the Beatles' arrival in the United States, said, "The British invasion this time goes by the code name *Beatlemania*." He meant that unlike soldiers during the Revolutionary War, this time it would be British music that was arriving to win the hearts of American fans.

By the mid-1960s, many performers from Great Britain had become wildly popular in the United States. The Beatles, the Rolling Stones, Herman's Hermits, the Dave Clark Five, Dusty

Michelle Obama born

The US Congress passes the Civil Rights Act on July 2, 1964

1964

Springfield, and the Animals all combined British and American music styles, fashion, and culture and brought them to the States.

Beatlemania described the intense fan devotion to the band and all things Beatle-related. It lasted from 1963 until the band broke up in 1970.

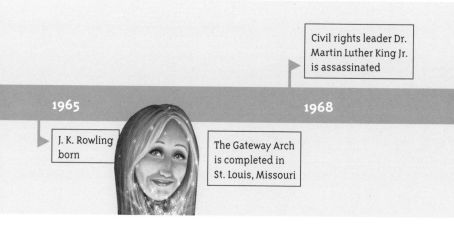

Civil rights leader Dr. Martin Luther King Jr. is assassinated

1965

1968

J. K. Rowling born

The Gateway Arch is completed in St. Louis, Missouri

Woodstock

From August 15 to August 18, 1969, nearly half a million people attended "3 days of Peace & Music," also known as the Woodstock Music and Art Fair. Thirty-two performers played outdoors on a farm in New York State over a weekend that came to define an entire countercultural generation of young people.

> Counterculture: A way of life that's opposed to—and often rejects—what is accepted as "normal" by more mainstream society.

Neil Armstrong becomes the first human to set foot on the moon

Sesame Street debuts on PBS

1969

The diverse Woodstock lineup included Ravi Shankar, Jimi Hendrix, Janis Joplin, Joan Baez, Santana, the Grateful Dead, Richie Havens, Arlo Guthrie, Jefferson Airplane, and Crosby, Stills, Nash & Young.

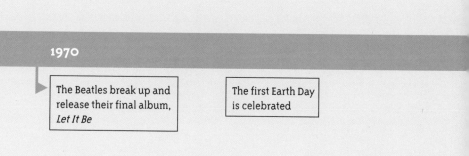

1970

The Beatles break up and release their final album, *Let It Be*

The first Earth Day is celebrated

Ms. Magazine

In 1971, Gloria Steinem and Dorothy Pitman Hughes cofounded *Ms.*, a magazine that was to be a voice *for* women, created *by* women. The magazine promoted feminism in all aspects of our culture.

Feminism: supporting women's rights and equality

Jeff Kinney born

Selena born

1971

1973

US troops withdraw from Vietnam

Watergate

Televised hearings of the Watergate scandal began on May 17, 1973, and captivated the nation. A year earlier, men working to reelect President Richard Nixon had broken into the Democratic National Committee headquarters in the Watergate office complex. They were hoping to unearth secrets held by the Democratic Party. The hearings led to the impeachment process against—and eventual resignation of—President Nixon.

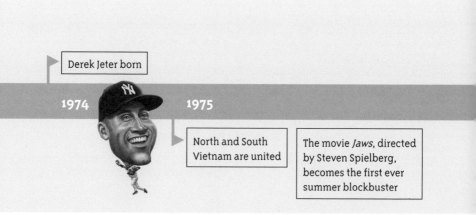

Derek Jeter born

1974   1975

North and South Vietnam are united

The movie *Jaws*, directed by Steven Spielberg, becomes the first ever summer blockbuster

The Soweto Uprising

In April of 1976, the Black students of Orlando West Junior School refused to go to school. They were protesting because the South African government had introduced Afrikaans—a form of the Dutch language that white settlers had brought to South Africa in the 1600s—as the standard language for subjects like math and science. Most Black schoolchildren could not understand Afrikaans. They preferred to be taught in English. Resistance spread throughout the region of Soweto. On June 16, 1976, around

Muhammad Ali defeats Joe Frazier in one of the greatest boxing matches of all time, known as the Thrilla in Manila, held in the Philippines

1975   1977

The world's first personal computer, the Commodore PET (Personal Electronic Transactor), is sold to consumers

twenty thousand students protested in the streets. The police responded with terrible violence, shooting directly into the crowd of children. Hundreds of people died that day, and thousands were injured. Because of the uprising, and the attention it drew from countries all over the world, the government of South Africa was forced to address its policy of apartheid. June 16 is now called Youth Day in South Africa in remembrance of the Soweto Uprising.

The apartheid system was one of racial separation (segregation) in South Africa. Although Black people were the majority of the population, they had very few rights. Only white South Africans, the minority, could vote. It was not until 1994 that the first democratic elections were held and Black citizens of South Africa could vote.

International soccer star Pelé retires

NASA space shuttle *Enterprise* makes its first test flight

May the Force Be with You

The opening of the movie *Star Wars*, in 1977, ushered in a new age of movie magic and storytelling. Writer and director George Lucas's tale of a galaxy far, far away was the beginning of a story that told of a new struggle between good and evil. The power of the Force, the energy that connects all things in the galaxy, is present in all life forms and is central to the Star Wars story.

For over forty years and across generations, the original *Star Wars*—now called *A New Hope*, or simply "IV"—has spawned its own empire of sequels, prequels, merchandise, and devoted fans all around the world.

The Wedding of the Century

On July 29, 1981, Lady Diana Spencer became the Princess of Wales when she married Prince Charles of England in a ceremony at Saint Paul's Cathedral in London. The world was captivated by every detail of the event, and an estimated 750 million people tuned in to watch it on television.

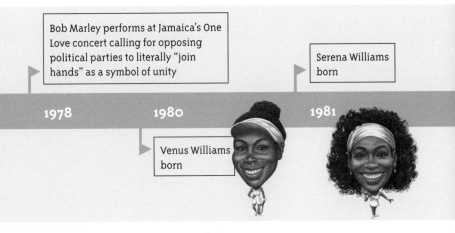

Bob Marley performs at Jamaica's One Love concert calling for opposing political parties to literally "join hands" as a symbol of unity

Serena Williams born

1978   1980   1981

Venus Williams born

The Fall of the Berlin Wall

On November 9, 1989, the Communist East German government announced that its citizens were free to visit West Berlin and West Germany for the first time since 1961. Crowds gathered to cross the border, climb the wall that divided the city, and to celebrate. They chipped away at the massive wall with tools and even their bare hands. Some people carried off chunks of the wall as souvenirs. The concrete section of the wall had been sixty-six miles long

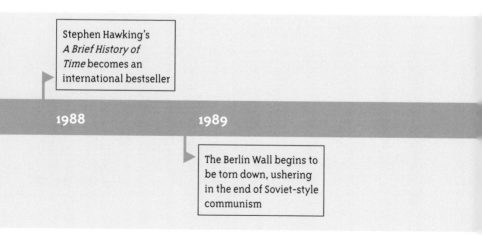

Stephen Hawking's *A Brief History of Time* becomes an international bestseller

1988   1989

The Berlin Wall begins to be torn down, ushering in the end of Soviet-style communism and over eleven feet high. It had divided a city and a nation for decades. The official demolition, completed by the German government, lasted from 1990 to 1992.

The "fall of the wall" led to the fall of communist governments across Eastern Europe, the collapse of the Soviet Union, and the end of the Cold War. This paved the way for the reunification of Germany—the uniting of the East and the West into one democratic nation—on October 3, 1990, what is now known as "Unity Day."

After twenty-seven years, Nelson Mandela is freed from prison in South Africa

1990

The World Wide Web is invented by Tim Berners-Lee

TY launches Beanie
Babies toys

Domestic terrorist Timothy
McVeigh bombs the
Murrah Federal Building in
Oklahoma City, killing 168
people

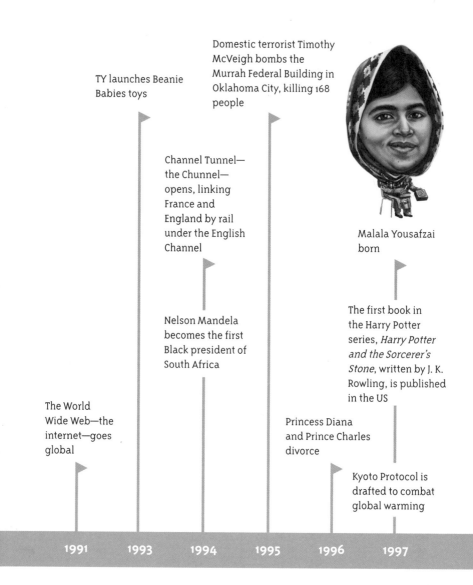

Channel Tunnel—
the Chunnel—
opens, linking
France and
England by rail
under the English
Channel

Malala Yousafzai
born

Nelson Mandela
becomes the first
Black president of
South Africa

The first book in
the Harry Potter
series, *Harry Potter
and the Sorcerer's
Stone*, written by J. K.
Rowling, is published
in the US

The World
Wide Web—the
internet—goes
global

Princess Diana
and Prince Charles
divorce

Kyoto Protocol is
drafted to combat
global warming

1991   1993   1994   1995   1996   1997

Google, the world's most popular search engine, is founded by Larry Page and Sergey Brin

Terrorists hijack four airplanes and crash them into the World Trade Center in New York; the Pentagon in Washington, DC; and a field in Pennsylvania on September 11

Oprah Winfrey becomes the first female African American billionaire

YouTube is launched

Y2K, the "Year 2000 Problem," was a computer bug that caused the year 2000 to be indistinguishable from the year 1900 in many digital systems

Hurricane Katrina devastates the US Gulf Coast, including New Orleans, Louisiana

Skype—voice over internet—is launched

Wikipedia is launched

| 1998 | 2000 | 2001 | 2003 | 2004 | 2005 |

Apple introduces
the iPhone

Sonia Sotomayor becomes
the first person of Hispanic
heritage to serve on the US
Supreme Court

Pakistani activist
Malala Yousafzai
is shot by Taliban
gunman; she survives

Barack Obama
becomes the first
African American
elected president
of the United
States

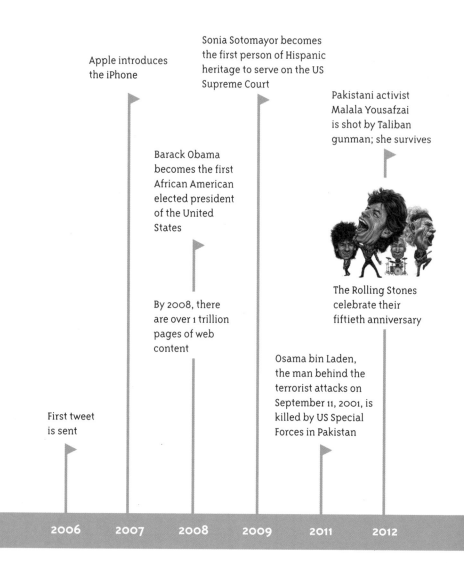

The Rolling Stones
celebrate their
fiftieth anniversary

By 2008, there
are over 1 trillion
pages of web
content

Osama bin Laden,
the man behind the
terrorist attacks on
September 11, 2001, is
killed by US Special
Forces in Pakistan

First tweet
is sent

| 2006 | 2007 | 2008 | 2009 | 2011 | 2012 |

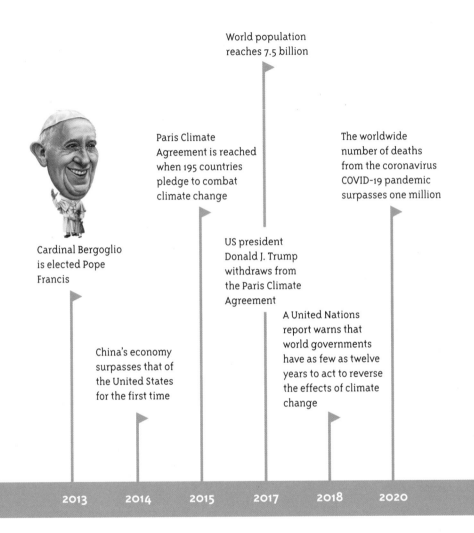

World population
reaches 7.5 billion

Paris Climate
Agreement is reached
when 195 countries
pledge to combat
climate change

The worldwide
number of deaths
from the coronavirus
COVID-19 pandemic
surpasses one million

Cardinal Bergoglio
is elected Pope
Francis

US president
Donald J. Trump
withdraws from
the Paris Climate
Agreement

A United Nations
report warns that
world governments
have as few as twelve
years to act to reverse
the effects of climate
change

China's economy
surpasses that of
the United States
for the first time

2013   2014   2015   2017   2018   2020

Bibliography

*Books for young readers

*Belviso, Meg, and Pam Pollack. *Who Was Alexander Hamilton?*
New York: Penguin Workshop, 2017.

*Belviso, Meg, and Pam Pollack. *Who Was Nelson Mandela?*
New York: Penguin Workshop, 2014.

DK. *Timelines of History*, 2nd ed. New York: DK Publishing, 2018.

*DK. *When on Earth?* 1st American ed. New York: DK Publishing,
2015.

*Fabiny, Sarah. *Who Was Fidel Castro?* New York: Penguin
Workshop, 2017.

Haugen, Peter. *World History for Dummies.* 2nd ed. Hoboken,
NJ: Wiley, 2009.

*McDonough, Yona Zeldis. *Who Was Harriet Tubman?* New York:
Penguin Workshop, 2002.

*Waterfield, Kathryn, and Robin Waterfield. *Who Was Alexander
the Great?* New York: Penguin Workshop, 2016.

*Workman Publishing. *Everything You Need to Ace American
History in One Big Fat Notebook*. New York: Workman, 2016.

*Workman Publishing. *Everything You Need to Ace World
History in One Big Fat Notebook*. New York: Workman, 2016.